THE HUMAN RIGHT

THE HUMAN RIGHT

Edited by Gina & Matt Bellomo

The Human Right
ISBN: 978-1-387-51751-0
Copyright © 2018 by Todd R Bishop

DEDICATED TO THE BROKEN.

WHAT OTHERS ARE SAYING

"The Human Right is a godly reminder of some of the things we take for granted as children of God. Too many times in our Christian walk, we forget all that has been done for us by Christ, and consequently, we live with stuff that the Savior has set us free from. This book will encourage you to grab hold of what is yours as a favored child of God!"

FRANK SANTORA

Lead Pastor - Faith Church, New Milford, CT

"If you're like me, you've probably grown up being told all the things that you're supposed to believe, like, God Loves You. But, maybe you've never embraced the reality of that truth. My great friend, Todd Bishop, in his new book, The Human Right, brings us face to face with the rights that belong to a Child of God. Many times we reject entitlements, because we think they only belong to those who have little value. But the truth is God has given "Rights" to those He calls His own. Pastor Todd, in a personal way, outlines these sometimes complex truths and makes them simple for anyone to understand and apply to their lives. You have the "right" to read this book... The Human Right!"

TIM CHAMBERS

Lead Pastor – Fresh Start Church – Egg Township Harbor, NJ

"This little book packs a big punch! Todd Bishop has given us a piece of himself and his stories will inspire you. In THE HUMAN RIGHT, Todd creates a lineup of critical truths that we all need to embrace. I highly recommend this book. Read it and live it - you will experience tremendous personal freedom and growth."

DAVID MARTIN

Your Success Coach and author of 12 TRAITS OF THE GREATS

"It's my honor to endorse my good friend Todd Bishop's book to you. What Todd has come from, to where he is today, is a testimony of the grace of our Lord. These "RIGHTS" of which he speaks are not "RIGHTS" that we demand of our Lord, but rather, these "RIGHTS" are freely offered to every believer, by Jesus. I encourage you to sit down and enjoy being reminded of what the Lord has already promised you."

RICH WILKERSON

Senior Pastor - Trinity Church, Miami, FL.

"Todd lives what He writes about. His insights in these pages speak life. His passion for Jesus and justice are transforming New York City and Long Island in a fresh and lasting way. As you encounter Jesus in Todd's new book, you will dream again and be filled with hope!"

JOHN BLONDO
Lead Pastor – Bethlehem Church, Richmond Hill, NY

"For many years, I've been privileged to know Todd Bishop as pastor, friend, and mentor. What Todd has been through, and how he has allowed God to radically refashion his life, is nothing short of the Creator's redemptive potential. The Human Right is a true work of art and a work of heart, written, not for the sake of self, but to empower YOU to take hold of YOUR God-given rights. Grabbing hold of these rights will revolutionize your life. There is no stopping you!"

GINA BELLOMO
Executive Pastor – Church Unleashed, Long Island, NY

"Todd Bishop is a true spokesperson for radical change. In The Human Right, he places a demand on our confidence; that it may rise. Not only does he share and make God's Good News relevant, but his life is an example of what he communicates to be our right to live the blessed life."

MARCUS GILL
Evangelist, Author & CEO – Marcus Gill International – Myrtle Beach, SC

"This book gives a raw and intimate look at the collision of the human condition coming in contact with the depth of God's compassion. It disarms the self-focused arguments of human insecurities while liberating the reader through the truth of the kingdom of God. It takes the reader on a journey of self-discovery leading them to freedom. It's a powerful expression of God's passionate pursuit toward His children. A must read for everyone who has ever struggled to be human."

KYLE HORNER
Lead Pastor – Connect Church, Cherry Hill, NJ

"At first blush, The Human Right reads like a personal memoir, and a great one it is. As you read deeper, you will discover that this book is a manual for renewal in the places that most people leave undone and wonder why, when they are in the presence of God, they are still undone. This book is an encouragement to practice the truth, so that we "come into the light, so that your deeds may be manifested as having been produced in God" (John 3:21). Todd is an instrument of healing. Read this, so that you too may be healed!"

CHARLES ROBERTS
Captain – The Salvation Army, Long Island, NY

"Joel Osteen and I consider Todd Bishop as a dear friend. We count it an honor to be doing life & ministry together through the Champions Network. This book carries a BIG message. Every issue one must face to succeed in life, Todd addresses in simple, yet pointed brilliance. You have a right to read and be forever impacted by this powerful book."

PHIL MUNSEY
Chairman – Champions Network at Lakewood Church – Houston, TX

"Todd Bishop has hit a home run with his latest book. He begins with a vulnerability not often seen in today's culture. He openly shares the struggle and brokenness he has experienced in his life, but he doesn't leave us discouraged and without hope. Instead, he takes us on a journey in which God delivers on His promise to provide each of us with what we need to experience real joy and purpose. In the chapter, "The Right to Dream", Pastor Todd challenges us to discard the label that others have placed upon us and to reach higher for the dream for which our heart yearns—and there is no greater example of this than Pr. Todd himself. If you are feeling alone, find yourself discouraged, or dealing with brokenness, then this is a must read!"

TROY GRAMLING
Lead Pastor – Potential Church – Cooper City, FL

"This book gives a raw and genuine view into what it's like to overcome in life. We all struggle for relevance and significance. Todd does a masterful job walking the reader towards freedom that can only be found in Christ. He reminds us through his own personal experiences that God's love is what leads us to our triumph."

BRANDON BALL

Lead Pastor – Church Unlimited – Birmingham, AL

"In a day and age where people hide behind nice appearances and good fronts, my great friend, Todd Bishop, does the unthinkable. He takes off the mask to reveal his true self in his new book, The Human Right. Todd's transparency and honesty is sure to touch your heart and transform your life. The Human Right helps us all to understand this universal truth: that our past does not and cannot terminate our God-given rights as His children."

JOSEPH NIEVES

Lead Pastor – Transformation Church – Middletown, NY

A BIG THANK YOU

There is no way I could ever write a book like this without the support of my family. My incredible wife, Mary, has been my greatest supporter, constant encourager, and most loyal friend. Thank you for allowing me to be me. My amazing kids, Malachi, Abigayl, and Bethany, may you always be God's voice to your generation. Each of you has been called by God for something great. I would not be who I am today with each of you. I love you all very much!

My mother, Judy, who taught me the value of hard-work, discipline, courage, and conviction. My two brothers, Kevin and Scott, I would not have survived growing up without you. Plus, you have given me some great sermon content over the years. We survived! My wonderful sister, Sarah, I am so glad that God brought you into my life!

My amazing family at Church Unleashed, which has become a place where dreams become reality. I am honored and humbled to lead such an incredible group of people. You all love me as I am, pray for me to be better, and support me as I am still growing.

My spiritual daughters, sons, nieces, and nephews you have taught me that my family is so much bigger. I am so grateful that you have allowed me to walk through life with you. Keep pursuing God. Never underestimate the power of hope.

CONTENTS

PROLOGUE

As a pastor who has now served in ministry for nearly 23 years, I have discovered that in every person there is something that wakes them up each day. Every individual ever created has something that drives their life, every single moment. For the single mom it is providing for her children. For the abused, it is protecting others. For the broken it is giving joy to those around them. Each person has something in them that pushes their intensity and drive to live. For me, it is the desire to make a difference in people's lives. It is to inspire others to dream bigger and believe for more.

Growing up was not always easy for our family. My parents were divorced when I was about two years old. It was a very challenging season for my mother as she raised three boys virtually on her own. She did an incredible job – the best she could. She worked long days and late nights to make sure her "boys" had everything they needed. My mother could not provide everything but she made sure we always had each other.

Even though my mother worked many hours and tirelessly served her family, she still needed some extra assistance. We were blessed to have grandparents who were able to assist, but we also had church food pantries and friends that would give us a shot in our arm when we needed it most. It was something I never admitted to my friends. I believe they knew it, but no one talked about it.

I did not see my father much. In fact, he was virtually non-existent. I remember the last thing we did together. We went to a Buffalo Bills game. I still remember the thermos we carried, the clothes I wore and how cold it was. I don't remember the score, but I do carry it as the best memory I have with my dad. That is probably because it is the only memory that I carry from my childhood.

For the next 10 years of my life I tried to understand why my family had so many struggles. I could not process it at the time, but I have learned how to process it today. I will never forget the times when we had barely enough to pay the bills and limited food in the fridge. The moments we would scrounge for change to put gas in the tank. It's hard to understand someone's struggle if you have not had that struggle. I have known struggle.

I questioned God. A lot. I doubted His plan. Often. If I am totally honest there were moments when I even hated Him. It is hard to admit today, but watching my mother go through her pain, agony, multiple divorces, and physical challenges would cause any young man to get frustrated.

4

I even blamed myself for my mother's challenges. I remember one time saying, "God, if I was never born, it would be so much easier for my mom." Tears are welling up in my eyes as I write this down because my leadership says, "Don't share it," but my love says, "Others must know."

I was broken. As a young man, I smiled on the outside, but was conflicted on the inside. I had suicidal thoughts often, poor self-worth, and negative inner dialogue routinely. I had private pain that was hard to verbalize to anyone else.

I needed to be loved.

I wanted to be me.

I desired to learn.

I hoped to be heard.

I dreamed of being respected.

I longed to be accepted.

I yearned for hope.

As a young man I was fragile. I remember transferring to a new school my freshman year of high school. One of the nicknames a few of the "popular kids" gave me was herpe face. Not the greatest way to make new friends. I had really bad acne around my mouth, but I just took the insults. I was used to being one of the poorest kids. I became accustomed to being treated differently than others.

God has given each of us rights. Human rights. He has placed in our DNA rights as His children. It is the human right to be loved, to be you, to be wrong, to be heard, to be respected, to be accepted and to dream. Those rights were kept from me growing up. I never felt like I could ever be anything, amount to anything or do anything.

Something changed the summer between freshman year and sophomore year of high school. I started working out. I began to gain a little weight. I decided to join the high school football team. I had always played pop-warner football growing up, so it was not a new thing for me, just a new school. I did not really fit in, but I really connected with my coach, Mike Masters. There was something different about him. He was the first person to ever push me. "Run, Bishop, Run." I have been running ever since. I think he was the first person outside of my family to invest in me, as a person.

So, why write this in the forward? It's very easy to look at where I am now and think, "He has no idea what I am going through." To some extent you will always be right. But, my prayer is that you will see that God can take the broken pieces of our lives and make something beautiful. I was a broken man. In many ways I still am. However, as I look back on all the broken pieces I endured I am grateful for each one. It has made me who I am today.

Scripture declares, "For God made human beings in his own image" (Genesis 9:6). I was made in the image of God. No one told me this growing up. Or maybe they did, but the pain blocked the message. Why was this not drilled into my spirit? I wish someone held me down and made me memorize this reality.

I have come a long ways since then, but this Buffalo-born boy still struggles at times with insecurity, feelings of failure, and negative inner dialogue. I still have a long way to go. We all do. As we discover our human rights, we will become all God designed us for.

This book is for the everyday, ordinary people who had a rough start, are going through difficulty, or are still living broken. Don't lose sight of your human rights!

THE RIGHT TO BE LOVED

Chapter 1

The most famous verse in the Bible says, "For God so loved the world that he gave his one and only son …" (John 3:16). The original word for world in this passage simply means "all of humanity."[1] So it would be better read, "For God so loved all of humanity that he gave his one and only son …" God created every person with the right to be loved. To be honest, I heard that Scripture my whole life, but I never believed it.

Growing up in church was great for many people, but not for me. I had a few good friends and enjoyed the youth events I attended. I played a good game. On the outside most people thought I was well adjusted. However, my inside was churning to find love. Don't get me wrong. There were times when I felt like God was standing next to me in Sunday services or weekly youth meetings. I had glimpses.

---

[1] Strong's Concordance. http://biblehub.com/greek/2889.htm

The phrase that the church tossed around all the time was "God is your loving Father." That burned me every time I heard it. Was it wrong? No. The challenge was that I was viewing the statement from the lens of my own experience. I could not understand the "Loving Father" concept because I did not have that. All I ever thought was, "Yea, I guess God will bail on me, like my father did." I never fought against the feelings. I struggled with God, as my Father. Everything in me wanted to embrace it, but my struggles kept me caged.

My grandfather, Leonard Janik, was one of my life heroes. He assumed the father-role in my life. He was a military man, a boxer, a railroad worker and the coolest old guy I ever knew. He smoked a pipe and to this day every time I get that smell in my nose I remember him. I always wanted to be around him. I longed for him to tell me that he loved me. I honestly do not ever remember hearing those words from him. He lost his battle with lung cancer in the mid 80's at 72 years old. Even today I wish I could here him say that to me.

Every person deserves to know they are loved. In fact, I believe every person needs to know it. The Bible teaches that "perfect love drives out fear" (1 John 4:18). That also means "no love creates fear." Those who feel unloved will often live with the fear of potential betrayal. As a pastor, for more than two decades I have experienced betrayal. We all do, but I am not going to let what one person does cause me to live in fear. I discovered God's love. It has removed the fear. When you discover real love fear is expelled.

I am so thankful that my mother told us often, 'I love you.' I don't think she ever missed a day. I can honestly say that one of my heroes growing up will always be my mother, Judith Bishop. She sacrificed her goals, dreams, and aspirations for her boys. She demonstrated real love. No matter how bad my day was or what I was going through, she always loved. When she beat my brothers with meat tenderizers it was out of love. The times she would embarrass us at football games it was out of love. The Christmases she would work overtime to have extra money to buy us a family gift it was all out of love. I saw God's love through my mom.

SOMETHING WAS MISSING.

I sought for peer approval. I worked harder at sports. I began to groom myself even more. I exercised 10 days per week (*yes, there are not 10 days in a week, but I doubled up a few days*). I started to play guitar. I did whatever I had to do find someone, anyone to approve of me. Yes, even not so positive things. I was trying to fill the void of "approval" with whatever would distract me from the lack. Nothing worked. Something was still missing.

God sent a youth pastor to my home church to reach me. I did not know it, he did not know it, but he was what I was missing. John Sotero was the first man I ever remember valuing and accepting me as me. Never once did "PJ" every try and change me. He accepted me as I was. John was also the first father figure that ever said, "I love you." Not in a weird way. Even though my mother was incredible, my spirit still cried out for a father to speak life into my brokenness.

Elijah, prophet in the Old Testament, was miraculously taken up into the heavens. His young apprentice, Elisha, was standing by watching. His leader is now gone. Elisha does not say, "My pastor, My pastor." He cries out in agony, "My father, My father." Every person, whether they admit it or not, needs a father in their life. Like me, a spiritual father will do.

OVERLOAD ON LOVE

There is not a conversation that goes by that I do not tell my wife, Mary, and our three amazing kids that I love them. Seriously, it's lover overload. It could be a 30 second conversation or a night out. It does not matter to me. I want everyone around me to know that I love them. I want them to hear those words. I don't want them to assume I do. I want them to know it.

One of the most important Scriptures on love is found in 1 John 4:7. It says, "... let us continue to love one another, for love comes from God. Anyone who loves is a child of God and knows God." Love comes from God. How insanely incredible is that reality? The essence of love is found in the one who created it. God overloads us with His love. When we struggle to find love and acceptance God is there. He lovingly and gently reminds us that we are loved.

There are many times in our lives when we need an injection of love. Too often we look to people as the number one source of love, but we can find ourselves disappointed. There is a void within all of us that only God can satisfy. If we can overload on God's love, He will fill every other desire for our lives. It all begins with the right to be loved by God.

Once I discovered God's love, my life took a radical turn. I still remember it like it was yesterday. It was my senior year of high school when I made the full on decision to pursue God. I had wavered back and forth, but in my senior year something clicked. I made the decision to trust God with my fragile heart. It was a decision I will never regret. It was the most important decision of my life.

A MISSION OF HOPE

I went off to Bible College seven months after this decision. Crazy, right, that I would jump right into my journey toward full-time ministry? Something in me always knew that I was called, but I ran as long as I could. It was many years after preaching to my GI Joe guys in the basement, but it finally came to life.

I believe God called me on a mission of hope because I know what it is to live hopeless. I want every person to know they are loved by God, and I want them to see His love through me. It is wrong for people to live unloved. Every person deserves to be loved – it is a human right. Gay or straight, rich or poor, man or woman, known or unknown – it does not matter. We must love people. It is our mission of hope.

Sadly, I don't think I was accepted at Bible College. I thought heading to a Christian college would eliminate some of the crap I dealt with growing up. It did not. Bible College was an incredible experience for me, but I always felt like the outsider. I did not have a "pastor-father" or "missionary-mother." It was just me. Yes, I had my brother, Kevin, go before me, but I still felt like the misfit. I don't imagine anyone intended to, but still I did. It was like high school all over again. You had the "cool" kids and then you had me.

Funny thing, many of the people who paid no attention to me in Bible college, now, all of a sudden, want to come preach at our church, send me texts, and reach out. Where was it when I needed it? I need love and acceptance. You see, that's what moves me. I know what it is to feel like the misfit, unknown, anti-social, and I want to make sure, to the best of my ability, to make sure no one around me feels like that. It is my mission to inspire hope.

LOVE IS MAGNETIC

I know for me that to feel love is to feel alive. When I first saw Mary, my wife, my heart skipped a beat. It's true. I remember going home after and calling my mother. I said, "Mom, today I met my future wife." We had barely spoken, but something attracted me to this Puerto Rican Princess. Now, here's the thing, she was not attracted to me! She thought I was brash, direct, and rude. All of which were probably true! But, she does admit that something in her knew, from the moment we met, that there was something special. That's because love is magnetic.

16

I've had my heart broken since I was a little kid. Little girls made fun of me when I was in elementary school. The youth group girls ignored me. The college girls messed with me. In fact, one girl even dumped me by email (That was messed up! We'll talk about that later.). But, now my heart was ready. I was ready. We were drawn together.

When God's love resides in our lives we will be magnetic to everyone around us. We must learn to love with no strings. Someone does not have to be perfect to be loved. They don't have to have it all together to be loved. We must commit to loving people regardless of whether they are right or wrong, Christian or non-Christian, perfect or flawed. Love will draw people to God.

Every person has the right to be loved by God and by us. Find someone today. Tell them you love them. Show them you care. Increase their value through love.

MESSY LOVE

It is easy to love people that are just like you. That's not difficult at all. Love is best seen when you love people that are different, unique or the exact opposite of who you are. You see, if you love those that are like you, then you are honestly only loving yourself. They are a picture of who you are. Real love is messy.

Love is not designed to just fit into a neat little box with a bow. It is fleshed out in real life. It is attached to hurts, pains, and difficulties.

Love is a beautiful mess that is best seen in people! Not just the people who are just like us, but in the forgotten and marginalized.

Love is the right of every person. Not just the affluent or famous. Love is not reserved solely for the heartthrob or bombshell. Love is for every single person that has ever been created by God.

When you love people that are not like you, it gets messy. You misspeak, because you don't understand their pain. You misunderstand, because you have not been in their situation. But that's the beautiful thing about love. It's messy. It's not designed to be captured in an Instagram post. It is designed to be lived out, given freely, and profoundly demonstrated by all to all. It is a right that all need!

CLAIM YOUR RIGHT

1. *What keeps you from sensing God's love?*

2. *Do you seek approval or love first? Why?*

3. *Who tells you they love you the most?*

4. *Who needs to hear "I love you" from you?*

I declare that I am loved by God, accepted by His grace, and kept by his promise. I claim my right!

THE RIGHT TO BE YOU

Chapter 2

I grew up in Western New York. It's hard to nail down which city, because we moved several times. What a great place to grow up. I did not have a ton of friends, but the ones I had were so meaningful in my life. They accepted me as I was. They did not expect me to change or be their idea for my life.

One of those people was John Trifilo. This guy. I won't share the stories of how we would take pellet guns and shoot out the porch lights in the expensive areas of town. I definitely will not tell you about putting the K-Mart shopping carts on the front of our car racing toward the building hoping to slip that cart into the wall. I would never ever do that. But I will tell you that John and I were incredible friends. Even today he is the only one that I keep in touch with from youth group.

John had both parents still. Lived in a nicer part of town. He was blessed in many ways. I grew up the opposite side. John and his entire family never cared. His mother, Mary Trifilo, became like a second mom. I spent a lot of time at their home. No one ever tried to change me. They accepted me.

I am not sure about you, but I know that I can struggle with *my* version of me and *God's* version of me. We often see all of our failures, our shortcomings, our sins, our struggles, and our challenges instead of His grace, His forgiveness, His freedom, and His favor! God made me. He made me with purpose and potential. Every gift, talent and ability was placed there by God. He made me to be me.

Many people throughout the Bible faced this! Gideon tried to resist God's call. Sarah and Abraham literally laughed at God's promise. Jeremiah offered God every excuse why he could not do what God called him to. Every person who desires to excel in this life will be faced with doubts. But, hear this today: "There will be times when we may want to be someone else – but don't cave in." God made you to be you. Someone once said, "If you and I are identical than one of us is unnecessary." You have the right to be you.

Scripture declares, *"All the days planned for me were written in your book before I was one day old"* (Psalm 139:16 - NCV). That means you can be who God designed you to be. You have the right to be the best you that you can be. God has plans for your life and they pre-date your birthdate. That means they can outlive anything that life or Hell throws at you! Before you were born, God created plans for your life! Is that not crazy? God has bigger plans for your life than you do!

See yourself through the way God sees you! Too many of us, when we look in the mirror of our lives, see the wrong image and the wrong person. We get down and discouraged about who we are and we fail to see who God made us to be. He broke the mold when He made us. There will never be another me. There will never be another you. Be the best you that you can be.

GET THAT HAT OFF

My mother tried several churches as we were growing up. She desired to find one that would best connect with her boys. She finally found one I think we all liked. It had good music, great people, and friendly pastors. My mother got my older brothers, Kevin and Scott, into the youth group. She got me plugged into their young boys program. It was a great experience.

One summer day I was wearing a hat in church. I did not know any better. An usher came up from behind, flicked off my hat and said, "Have some respect in God's House." Ouch. At eleven years old, this turned me off. I could not believe that someone, who did not even know me, would do that. I was just being me. Even today I am still a hat-wearing guy.

The message that was sent to me that day was "God doesn't want you the way you are He wants you the way we want you to be." From that point on, for years, I would skip church. John and I would go to the local convenient store, buy a candy bar, and sit in one of our parent's cars. We liked John's mom's car. It was a red Cadillac with white interior, much better than my mom's Ford Escort Wagon.

It was the first time I felt rejected by a church. I never had that feeling before. That's probably why I am the way I am today. I don't really care how someone comes to church, I just want them to come. I want people to come as they are, to place their lives in the hands of God, and watch God build their lives. God hard-wired in all of us the right to be us.

STIFF NIPPLE

Did I get your attention? I have always loved music. I love to listen to it and play it. Music is an escape, but it is also an experience. It allows you to dream and hope. Music helped me to find a separation from where my life was. I used music to take me to another place. It was what I needed. At that time, church music was not the greatest thing happening. To be honest, most of it was barely tolerable.

I really loved Heavy Metal music. In fact, I still do. I listened to everything with a fast sound, driving guitars, and insane drum cadences. We did not have iPods, iPhones, or iPads back then, but we did have Walkman's. If you don't know what a Walkman is, you don't know the struggle. A Walkman was a portable CD player with headphones. A 16-Gig iPhone can hold about 4000 songs. That would be about 300 CD's you would have to carry with you.

My mother only wanted us to listen to Christian music. So I had some of that too. If she saw a non-Christian CD, she would break it and throw it in the garbage. She was hard-core. I would still sneak in Metallica, Twisted Sister, Black Sabbath, Pantera and more. I got my first guitar at 12 years old and continued my love for music. I went from listening to playing. I enjoyed music, but I loved to play it. I was not, and still am not, the greatest guitarist, but my love for music has continued to grow.

What does all this have to do with Stiff Nipple? Here we go. In my senior year of high school I used to be in a garage band with a couple of guys. It was a punk band. We called it – wait for it – you guessed it – Stiff Nipple. We just loved music. We played covers in my friend's house. I have never shared that band title publicly until now. No one in church knew back then. My mother did not know and she is probably freaking out right now. It was a place for me to be me. I never shared it because I knew no one, at that time, would accept it. I had to hide me.

FAKE AIN'T YOUR FUTURE

Too many people settle for being what they are not. They allow culture to label them, society to direct them, and people to change them. The Bible declares, "For we are God's masterpiece. He has created us anew in Christ Jesus, so we can do the good things he planned for us long ago" (Ephesians 2:10). It became the anthem verse of my life. I am God's masterpiece.

For a long time I tried to be someone else's carbon copy. I faked my spiritual life, faked my happiness, faked my dreams and became a fake me. I became a chameleon. I blended in wherever I was. It took me a long time to realize that there is only one Todd Bishop and that's who I was designed to be.

YOU are God's masterpiece. Log in to Facebook right now and post, "I am God's masterpiece." Now hashtag it #TheHumanRightBook. It's a simple, yet profound reality. You were made by God for a divine purpose! You are not junk, left-overs or crap. You are a one-of-a-kind piece of art that God designed to leave your mark on this world.

Refuse to believe the lies that I believed growing up. "You are not good enough." "No one cares." "If you died, it would not matter." Stand on the declaration of God's Word, "I am God's masterpiece." You are not a failure, mistake or an accident. You made by God to be you. Be the best you that you can be! Fake ain't your future.

BE YOU

God made you. That's a difficult thing to grasp, but he formed you with his words. You see, long before you were conceived in the belly of your mother you were conceived in the heart of God. He did not design you to run someone else's race. He formed you with a specific design. Your skills, talents and abilities were given to you by God. Your eye color was specifically picked out by God. Not a detail of your life was left untouched by God. His fingerprints are all over your DNA.

Refuse to get consumed with keeping up with everyone, trying to be someone you are not. It's exhausting and it gets old. Wake up everyday and declare, "I am going to be the best me that I can be." Don't live to make other people happy. Live to please an audience of one – God. If He is happy with you, then it does not matter who is unhappy with you. You have the right to be you!

CLAIM YOUR RIGHT

1. *Do people's opinions affect you? Why or why not?*

2. *What labels about you do you need to change?*

3. *Have you ever been a fake you? If so, how?*

4. *Do you believe you are God's masterpiece?*

I declare that God accepts me as I am, makes me who I need to be, and guards me as I grow. I claim my right!

THE RIGHT TO BE WRONG

Chapter 3

I have made many mistakes over my lifetime. Too many to count and way too many to admit. Our mistakes are proverbial reminders of how God wired our lives. He did not create robots who would be fully compliant or servants who would have no say in their choices. Instead, God gave you and I the right to choose.

Adam and Eve were given the right to choose. Think about it. God created them, placed them in a garden dream and provided everything for them. He also gave them the right to be wrong. He told them they can eat of any tree in the Garden of Eden, except one, The Tree of The Knowledge of Good and Evil. Long story short, the serpent tempts them and they end up eating what they were told not to.

Before we go postal on Adam and Eve, let me ask you a question. How many times do we go and do exactly the opposite of what God says? Don't have sex until you are married – people still do it. Don't want what others have – we still want it. Don't murder – we still kill babies by record amounts. Don't lie – everyday someone is lying to somebody about something. God has given to each of us the right to be wrong.

The Bible reveals, "Temptation comes from our own desires, which entice us and drag us away. These desires give birth to sinful actions. And when sin is allowed to grow, it gives birth to death" (James 1:14-15). God placed in us the ability to choose. That is one of the most incredible traits of our Creator. He did not want us to serve Him by force but by choice! Life tempts us. What we do with those temptations is up to us.

WHO IS IN CHARGE

A pastor friend of mine (*much more like a spiritual father*), David Nuzzolo, said one time, "What's right or wrong? Well, that depends on who is in charge." That is so true. Whoever is in charge makes up the rules. The speed limit is 65 MPH, but you choose to go 85 MPH. A police officer pulls you over and asks, "Do you know why I pulled you over?" Your response, "No officer." He says, "You were speeding." You then explain to him that 85 MPH was the speed limit you chose for today. He is still going to give you that ticket. Why? You are not the authority over the speed limit!

I love this passage of Scripture, it says, "What sorrow awaits those who argue with their Creator. Does a clay pot argue with its maker? Does the clay dispute with the one who shapes it, saying, 'Stop, you're doing it wrong!' Does the pot exclaim, 'How clumsy can you be?'

(Isaiah 45:9). What's right or wrong? It depends on who is in charge. If you believe, like me, that God is our authority then His rules, plans and purposes are always right.

Imagine, as a student, going to your professor and saying, "I am not going to do that assignment, because I am in charge of my life." His response will be something like this: "You may be in charge of your life, but I am in charge of your grades." Life teaches us that someone has to be in charge. I wonder how many times we are making up our own rules at the speed of life and God is up in Heaven saying, "Seriously, I told you not to do that because I want to protect you from pain."

Mary, our kids, and I went to BLAZE Pizza one night. I noticed one of their slogans written on the wall, "UNFOLLOW THE RULES." I thought. "Perfect, I am going to unfollow the rules and not pay." So when I suggested to the young lady behind the register that I didn't have to pay, we both realized that 'Unfollow The Rules' is a great slogan, but not the reality.

THERE'S THE DOOR

My mother tried to keep us from doing bad things. This was no easy task. Raising three boys to make right choices could be challenging. My mother made the rules. It was her house. I remember one of my brothers doing something wrong. She caught him and said, "If you don't like my rules there's the door." What she was saying is that this is the way it is. You are entitled to do what you want, but that does not mean I have to allow it in my house.

God has given each person a 'free-will.' That is simply the ability to choose for themselves whether or not they will do the right thing. Now, growing up in church, I thought that any time I made a mistake I was going to Hell. It's true. I must have booked a one way trip, in my mind, every day growing up. I blew it a lot. I was raised in a spiritual environment where I thought God was up in Heaven saying, "If you don't like my rules there's the door."

I grew up in a "letter of the law" church. Not much grace. There was very little room for people to be human. The result was I never thought I would measure up. If I am going to blow it repeatedly and often, why even try? So in my early teens, I stopped trying. Yes, I still went to church, but church became more of a "to do" list. To be perfectly honest, I could not keep up with that list.

A PICTURE OF GRACE

I did not really understand grace until I was in Bible College. I won't go into great details, but I was almost suspended my senior year. It was something so foolish, but there was a new Dean of Men and he wanted to make sure his authority was established. I get it. He wanted me kicked out. That would have been extremely devastating for me, my mother, and our family.

I was called into the Dean of Students office, Gary Bruegman. He told me the punishment recommended to him. I was so scared. Then he said, "Todd, I see too much potential in you. I am not going to kick you out." I could not believe it. He did not say, "There's the door." Gary said, "Here's grace." I never fully understood God's grace until that day. I deserved to be shown the door, but I was given grace. Yes, I have the right to be wrong and to make my choices. Still, God has the right to forgive and extend grace.

1 John 1:9 declares, "But if we confess our sins to him, he is faithful and just to forgive us our sins and to cleanse us from all wickedness." I admitted my failure. I accepted responsibility. Grace was given. Forgiveness was extended. A life, mine, was shown a true picture of God's grace.

YOU CAN'T EARN IT

Here's what I have learned: "Your hope does not rest on what you do – but in what Jesus has done." If it's on us, we are going to screw it up. Man can never get it right. The Bible says, and this is huge, "For no one can ever be made right with God by doing what the law commands. The law simply shows us how sinful we are" (Romans 3:20). Your behavior can never make you right with God. Why? Because our behavior is often not good! In fact, it is wrong. A few verses later we are told what makes us right with God: "So we are made right with God through faith and not by obeying the law" (Romans 3:28). That means you can't earn God's grace.

Have you ever lied? Cheated? Stolen anything? On our own we are lying, cheating thieves. So we cannot do enough good to erase all our bad. That's why God sent His Son to be the Supernatural Sin Eraser. To remove our sins and do what we could never do, so we could become what He designed us to be. God has given each of us the right to be wrong, but He has the right to make us right no matter what we have done.

Too many people go through life trying to earn God's love. If I pray more, give more, or read the Bible more, God will accept me. This is hard to grasp but God will not love you any more or any less than He does right now. Even when we are wrong, we blow it, or we make major mistakes, God still loves us.

SUCKER SYNDROME

Growing up without my father in my life left many voids. However, I discovered it also did something powerful. It motivated me to give my kids everything that was kept from me. I have what I call 'Sucker-Syndrome.' It may not be a true medical disorder, but I do have it. Sucker Syndrome is the incapacity to not give your kids something. If I go to the store and one of my girls says they want something, I can say "no," at first. Then they give me the look, and I walk out of the store with everything I did not want. Then, I have to explain to Mary why my girls got another doll.

You see, my kids do not have to earn my love by being perfect. They have it no matter what. They don't have to earn it. Yes, they are going to make mistakes. I don't want them to,

teacher mistakes are. So my kids have the ri

have the responsibility to correct them. The s

have the right to be wrong and God has the resi

me.

If I don't correct my kids when they are wrong, it actually devalues them. It reveals my lack of concern for their decisions, life, and future. The Bible says, "No discipline is enjoyable while it is happening--it's painful! But afterward there will be a peaceful harvest of right living for those who are trained in this way" (Hebrews 12:11). The right to be wrong must also have as a companion the right to be corrected.

CLAIM YOUR RIGHT

1. *What authority are you under? Yours or Gods?*

2. *Is there a mistake you made that you still regret?*

3. *Where do you need to receive God's forgiveness?*

4. *Is there a place where you need God's correction?*

I declare that I am forgiven by Jesus, freed by the cross, and righteous by His love. I claim my right!

THE RIGHT TO BE HEARD

Chapter 4

No other generation in our history has been given such an immediate platform. Social media has changed the landscape of communication. This generation wants to be heard. They want their voice to make a difference. Political, religious, and societal leaders are trying to silence this generation. That is a huge mistake.

My heart is broken as I look across our nation. Our nation has become divided over hashtags of hate, distasteful tweets, and shameful Youtube videos. I am not one to get involved in political pontification or social activism or divisive debate, but I cannot be silent when our nation is so divided. I cannot sit by, watch, and not say anything.

The truth is, it would be easier for me to be silent and to not address the issues of our day, but God has given every generation the right to be heard. As I share my heart, some will misunderstand, others may put words in my mouth, some may get frustrated I don't say enough and still there will be those who say " You said too much." Even so, I cannot be silent.

God has given me a voice, a platform. To not use it would be an injustice. God has called me to speak up for those who cannot speak up for themselves. He has called me to stand with those who have been marginalized, neglected, and ignored. Every person has the right to be heard.

THE MAN OF PEACE

Jesus. A man of peace and love. He came to this world with ONE mission – to bring people back into a right relationship with God. Jesus healed the sick, opened the eyes of the blind, raised the dead, and encouraged everyone.

He was insulted.

He was attacked.

He was arrested.

He was tortured.

He was crucified.

Not by the enemy, but by those, who just one week earlier, were shouting his praises. Jesus knows what it means to be betrayed. There are a lot of people today who feel betrayed. Jesus knows what it is like to be murdered. There are many who experienced that in the circle of relationships. Jesus knew injustice, prejudice, pain, manipulation, and everything in between. Scripture declares, "This High Priest of ours understands our weaknesses, for he faced all of the same testings we do, yet he did not sin" (Hebrews 4:15). Jesus knows what we experience, because he walked that journey before us.

Dr. Martin Luther King Jr was not silent on the issues of his day. It affected his life. His stance ended his life but his words still ring out, "We must learn to live together as brothers or perish together as fools."[2] There are so many issues that can divide us if we let them, but there is so much more we have in common.

Mary and I lead a diverse church. I believe that's because we have tried to love everyone equally. We have not placed certain people above others. We work hard to make sure that everyone feels loved and valued. John 13:35 declares, "Your love for one another will prove to the world that you are my disciples ..."

Hate speech. Violent actions. Negative posts about cops or blacks – or any other group – devalues people and de-validates our beliefs. Love. It's what I know best and should show the most. My heart breaks for the world we are giving to the next generation. Let's be people of peace. Let's seek unity over uniformity. There is no way that we can be the answer that humanity needs when we are stuck in a personal

---

[2] https://www.brainyquote.com/quotes/martin_luther_king_jr_101309

struggle. His peace must be our priority. Follow the man of peace and you will become a person of peace!

AN HONEST RANT

Jessica came to our church several years ago. I remember some of our early conversations. "I don't know if I could ever sit under a white preacher as my spiritual leader." Not a good way to begin our journey. If you haven't figured it out, Jessica is black. She has faced prejudice, insults, and more during her lifetime. So I can understand her apprehension. I think in one of our early conversations, I told her, "I am black on the inside." She politely laughed.

Jessica kept coming to the church, but you could feel the disconnect. Then something happened. The emergence of Black Lives Matter, Blue Lives Matter and All Lives Matter movements surged to the front of the press. Many in our nation were frustrated by what they perceived as a broken system. The law enforcement officers were being gunned down in our streets. 2016 was a very difficult year.

As a pastor, I could not sit by and say nothing. I preached a message called, "I Cannot Be Silent." I was not sure how it would be received, but I followed my heart. At the very end of the message, I washed the feet of an officer and a person of color. In all services, all of us wept, embraced, and used our right to be heard. We spoke a solid message of unity.

At the end of that service Jessica came up to me. Pride in her spirit, slights tears in her eyes, and said, "Today, you became my pastor." This was one of the happiest days of ministry I have had. Jess spoke and I listened. I spoke and she listened. The right to be heard was married to the responsibility to listen.

I want to apologize to you, on behalf of all leaders – political, spiritual and institutional - for the verbal assaults, attacks, and accusations that supposed authorities throw at each other all the time. I want to say I am sorry for the immature, incompetent leaders who will not respect the rights of others to be heard. Leaders who cannot listen should not lead.

SILENTLY COMPLICIT

There is no way that you can be a Christian and be a racist. These words will never fit together. Racism is the byproduct of hatred. To treat someone differently, because of skin color is a slap in the face of our creative God, who created every nation, every tribe, and every race.

In the early 1900's, there was a move of God that broke out in a place called Azusa Street in Los Angeles, CA. Blacks, Whites, Latinos, Asians, and other races got together for one reason. Jesus! Frank Bartlemen, a Pentecostal writer, preacher, and missionary wrote about

Azusa Street, "The color line was washed away in the Blood [of Christ]."[3]

I will never forget my junior year of high school. It was predominantly a white school. There was very limited diversity. Our football team, which I played for, had only one black player, LaDarian. It was not called often, but our quarterback, during practice, would call "X-99" from the line of scrimmage. It was an audible. What was X-99? That's when our quarterback would intentionally throw an interception to LaDarian and the offense would tackle him. I never dove in for the tackle, but I stood by. Something I now regret.

I think that's why I speak up. I will never again be the 16-year old kid who is complicit by silence. So let me be loud and clear. Racism exists. It should be always be condemned. No one should ever be judged by the color of their skin, where they grew up, or who their parents are. We should see each other as beautifully made by a wonderful God.

A MODERN DAY GENOCIDE

Over 60 million children have been killed by abortion since 1973.[4] It is a truly staggering number. A number that should break our hearts. As a pastor, I have had many conversations with women who have

---

[3] http://www.pentecostaltheology.com/azusa-the-color-line-was-washed-away-in-the-blood/
[4] http://www.lifenews.com/2018/01/18/60069971-abortions-in-america-since-roe-v-wade-in-1973/

had abortions. It is something that most still live with an overwhelming guilt. Not all, but most.

My mother was not sure she would be able to have children. She survived a very difficult battle with polio as a child. It affected much of her body. She still bares scars on her body from experimental procedures. She actually conceived five babies, but only three survived. One of the babies she conceived had many complications. During delivery the doctors determined to medically abort the baby. They did not believe the child would survive delivery. This moment still brings my mother to tears.

I wonder what dreamers, inventors, politicians, pastors, innovators, teachers and missionaries were never given the chance to fulfill their destiny. It seems as though the enemy has tried to wipe out an entire generation. The sacred view I have of life compels me to speak up for those who cannot speak up for themselves. Every child has the right to be born.

GREATEST ACT OF HATE

Jesus is forecasting his crucifixion. He says this, "And when I am lifted up from the earth {*in other words, when I have been placed on the cross unjustly to die in your place*}, I will draw everyone to myself" (John 12:32). Circle the word everyone. The word everyone comes from the original Greek word, πᾶς (pas), meaning EVERY

KIND.[5] Jesus did not die for one kind, He died for every kind of person; not just one group, but all groups; not just perfect people, but imperfect people.

Jesus was arrested, convicted, and condemned. Have you been mistreated? Jesus knows. Lied about? Yep, He was there too. Here's what I discovered about Jesus' crucifixion: *The biggest act of hate in human history has resulted in the greatest movement of love*! Jesus is all about love. Let's keep the movement of love going and growing strong.

I will not put my hope in government. I will not put my trust in education. I cannot place my confidence in our military. I place my hope and trust in Jesus Christ. Jesus is truly the answer. He is the great unifier. He is the one that can bring us together. We cannot keep taking Jesus out of the public square, out of our schools, out of our political gatherings, out of our society, and expect better results.

We need a move of God. We need the presence of Jesus to be evident. Jesus is the only answer for society's problems. We don't need less of Jesus, we need more of Him! We don't need more information or more education. We need more transformation, and that only comes through the person of Jesus.

Every person has the right to be heard. The Bible declares, "...we know he hears us when we make our requests," (1 John 5:14). Don't miss this. God hears you! He listens to your cries in pain and He

---

[5] Strong's Concordance. http://biblehub.com/greek/3956.htm

hears your celebration of praise! There is not one word that you speak or think that God does not pay attention to. He has given you the right to be heard and He is always listening.

CLAIM YOUR RIGHT

1. Have you ever felt your voice was silenced?

2. Where does your hope and trust come from?

3. Are there any changes you need to make to secure your hope and trust in Christ?

4. Is there an injustice that needs you voice?

I declare that I will use my voice for the marginalized and forgotten. I will not be silent. I claim my right!

THE RIGHT TO BE RESPECTED

Chapter 5

One of the most exciting things growing up was K-Mart's Blue Light Special. K-Mart would run these amazing deals. That's when my mom would shop for clothes, gifts, and more. She leveraged sales, coupons, and many "Blue Light Specials." If you don't know, now you know. While I admire my mom's thriftiness, which she learned from her mother, it created an affect that I never talked about.

Because we moved often I had to shift schools a lot. It wasn't easy. My mother tried public school and Christian school. She hoped that we would fit in. I think my brothers fit in better than me. One of the schools we transferred to was extremely difficult at first. It got better, but I remember a few of the students calling me "White Trash." I still don't know why, but it was brutal.

It seemed as though everywhere I went growing up, I faced people who disrespected me without knowing me. That is the big problem in our culture today. We trivialize what we make no time for. We minimize those who we don't waste a minute on. As a young man, I longed to be respected. I needed it.

I learned a lie growing up: Respect is earned. I was taught that you can't just expect people to respect who you are or what you do. You have to earn it. It was drilled in my head at home, school, and even church. I have to live my life with such excellence that people say, "Now, that's someone I can respect." This flies in the face of Scripture. "Respect everyone, and love your Christian brothers and sisters. Fear God, and respect the king" (1 Peter 2:17).

Respect is not earned. It is a right.

COMPETITION

I have long believed that competition reveals character. It exposes what lies beneath the surface of someone's life. Have you ever noticed how irate parents get at sports events? It's crazy. They scream at officials, yell at their kid's coaches, and event get in fist fights with other parents. Not that respectful.

In our hopes to push our children higher, we teach disrespect for authority and leadership. No one wakes up disrespectful. It is modeled before them. If you ever meet a disrespectful child, just wait till you meet their parents.

My mother used to come to all of our football games. I am not sure how she juggled long hours at work, rushing us to practice, and then

attending every game for all three of us. But, she did i
showed up with a BIG red megaphone. You cannot make this stuff
up! Here were some of her cheers: "C'mon Bishop, get 'em." "Break
their legs." "Make them pay." "Kill, Warriors, kill." Yep, it was
often embarrassing, but my mother did it mostly for comic relief. I
think.

Competition brings out the best in us, but it can also bring out the
worst. It almost seems as though sports have taught us you can be
one thing on the field and another thing off the field. I totally
disagree. No matter where we are or what we do, we must exemplify
godly character. We don't leave our God-Jersey in the locker room.
We take it with us wherever we go.

WHAT DO WE WANT: DEAD COPS.

I have the amazing privilege to have some of my greatest friends as
law enforcement officers. These guys work crazy hours, put their
lives on the line daily, and do it every time they strap on their shield.
In recent years, we have seen highly publicized police shootings.
Many justified. Others hard to watch. Police officers have an
incredibly difficult job. Split second decisions impact lives.

We were taught to respect people of authority. Every person. It did
not matter if we agreed with them, liked them, or even knew them. It
broke my heart a couple of years ago when the news showed
protestors chanting, "What do we want? Dead Cops. When do we

want them? Now." I thought of all the great officers, retired and active, that I know. My heart broke for these friends.

Let me say this, I am all about protesting, but protesting must be done in a way where the message is not missed due to poor behavior. My grandmother taught me growing up that two wrongs never make a right. Wrong is still wrong. We have been given the right to peaceful protest in our nation. It is a great right. It allows the people to be heard, but it is never right to protest in disrespect.

Our law enforcement officers should be respected. The vast majority are incredible people who are doing a fantastic job. In any occupation there will be people filled with hate, racism, bigotry, and malice, but that does not mean they all are. Let's not lump every person into the same category. That would be disrespectful.

MY FIRST PASTOR POSITION

The first church that took a risk on me was a little church in Hartford, New York. I was so excited about the opportunity to pastor my own church at 23 years old. It was a dream come true ... until. After I took the position, I discovered I was their 10th pastor in 10 years. I was immature. I did not ask a lot of questions. It was a small church in upstate New York. I truly believed God called me there.

I remember my first board meeting. It went pretty well. We spoke about one specific thing that a board member brought up and I spoke in opposition to the idea. After the meeting he pulled me aside, grabbed my elbow and said, "Get your s#^t together." I did not know what to say. I was speechless. That began the downward spiral.

A few months later they cut my salary. Then they cut it again. I felt disrespected, dejected and devalued. I would cry myself to sleep many nights during that process. I finally had enough. I called for a special board meeting. I asked my friend, Tim, to be at the meeting as an observer. I shared the 13 things that needed to change for me to remain their pastor. They said, "No," to all thirteen things. I handed them my resignation.

After we left, Tim said to me, "Todd, you have some big ones." I could not believe he said that, but that's what he said. This is a no filter book. He went on to say that it is "impossible to serve people that don't respect you." How true is that? Respect has become a lost right in our world today. Everyone deserves to be respected.

A LESSON IN HONOR

A woman in the Bible is living an adulterous life. Insane right? Caught in the very act, she is then brought to the middle of the village to be stoned. That was the punishment in Jesus' day. Jesus is then asked, "Teacher, what should be do." He stoops down and begins to draw in the dirt. His simple, yet profound response, "All right, but let the one who has never sinned throw the first stone" (John 8:7). The Bible reveals that, one by one, they all dropped their stones and left. Jesus' final words to this woman, "I won't condemn you. Go and don't return to that lifestyle" (*My paraphrase*). This woman, according to the law, deserved punishment, but Jesus chose to honor.

Those who don't deserve honor should still be given honor. There are always going to be people in our lives who do not live honorably, but that does not mean they should be dishonored. Every person is given the right to be respected. Not because they always deserve it, but because God desires it.

Honor. It is the lost art of our world today. The Bible declares, "Love each other with genuine affection, and take delight in honoring each other" (Romans 12:10). Let's focus on the last statement, "take delight in honoring each other." The word honor simply means, "assigning value."[6] Take delight in adding value to someone's life and show them what they are worth. Declare how much they mean to you and to others. It should make us happy to honor others.

Do you know when we tend to honor people? When they are in a coffin or casket. Man, that's too late to show honor. We should show honor to the people that are around us, that love us, value us, and believe in us. We should even honor those who don't like us, talk about us, attack us and abandon us.

RESPECT ME

Our culture has quickly lost its ability to respect people. It seems like no one knows how to respect anyone. Respect is not that difficult. I

---

[6] Strong's Concordance. http://biblehub.com/greek/5092.htm

grew up believing that we should treat others the way we hope they treat us. Respect should not have to be demanded or earned. It is a right.

The world needs to learn how to respect again. No one should have to scream, "Respect me." It should be something that we love to give to people. Respect should be seen in politics, churches, schools, and sporting events. Respect should be given to all. It should never be based on race, gender, beliefs, or religion. Every person deserves to be respected.

Jesus Christ, the person of highest honor, came down to us, the people of lowest honor, and gave us what we did not deserve, but what we needed – HONOR. Take delight and be like Jesus. Honor someone today. It is their right.

CLAIM YOUR RIGHT

1. Do you feel you have to earn respect?

2. Why do you feel that most people believe that respect is earned?

3. No matter your experience which person (or people) deserve your respect today?

4. Take it one step further, who can you honor today?

I declare that respect is the right I must not only possess, but give. It is a gift. I claim my right!

THE RIGHT TO DREAM

Chapter 6

I have always been a bit of a dreamer. I think it started as I attempted to escape the difficult realities of my early years. I dream about everything. In fact, sometimes I need someone to bring me back to reality. Too often I live with my head in the clouds, but I believe that those who stop dreaming eventually stop living. God has given every person the right to dream.

All throughout the Bible, you discover that God used dreams to speak to people, direct nations, and confirm destinies. I believe God still uses dreams. Now, we have to be cautious, because sometimes we base our lives on dreams that were never from God. This happens all the time. I remember serving in my second church in Hudson Falls, New York, Gospel Lighthouse Church, when a well meaning woman told me she had a dream about a can of 7*Up. She asked, "Pastor, what did it mean?" I quickly responded, "Seven is the number of completion – you are complete in Christ. The red dot symbolizes the blood of Christ – you are covered. The "up" means that you are going up when Jesus comes." She looked at me with awe. Then I told her the truth, "Maybe you were just craving a 7*Up."

Dreams can be very tricky to navigate. I know that Mary and I, when we first met, both wanted to land, eventually, in Tennessee. It was a marker God used to confirm our relationship. About 6 years into our marriage we started praying about what God had in store for our lives next. We felt the strong tug at our spirits that we were going to start a new church. Immediately, we assumed it would be in Tennessee. However, God had different plans for our lives. We began a prayer journey that would lead us to discover that God wanted us to plant a church on Long Island. This just got real.

We wanted our dream, but God had a slightly different dream. Our future often is a collision between our dreams and God's. Mary and I discovered early that, if we want to be the happiest, we must adapt our plans to God's.

HUMANITY DREAMS

He placed in all of humanity the right to dream. It could be the young boy who dreams of playing basketball in the NBA. It could be the young girl who dreams of being a princess or the single mom who dreams of landing the perfect job. It could even be the person who wants to create a cure for a disease. Every person who was ever created had dreams.

Where did the right to dream come from? It came from God. Remember, He is the one who dreamed of earth, humanity, animals, and all that came into existence with just the words, "Let there be ..." Those words are still creating today. Everything you taste, touch, smell, feel, and see is the result of God's dream coming to life. We were made in His image. That means we have the capacity to bring dreams to life too.

I believe that dreams that are never attempted become nightmares of missed opportunities. At the end of our lives, I believe our greatest regrets may be the things we never attempted, tried, or went after. There are so many people that share their dreams, but they never walk them out. They dream, but they do not act. True dreamers put their faith where their dreams are. They try things and fail. Then they try again.

Dreams are what keep us awake at night and motivate us to get up in the morning. Dreams fuel your hope, lift your spirit, and inspire your life. God has placed within each of us the capacity to dream. Never settle for the life you never wanted. Bust out of that shell. Dream again. It is your right.

DON'T WEAR THE LABEL

My senior year of Bible College I was on the cheerleading squad. Yes, it's true. I was a cheer lifter. I had filled in because someone was kicked out of school, so they were short one person. I jumped in to help. At the end of the year, I was given a portfolio. It had some pictures and people wrote notes. The last page had a "where will you be in 10 years" section. The team wrote, "Pastoring a small church in a rural town." That bothered me.

When I got home I tossed that portfolio in the garbage. It hurt deeply, because that's what my peers thought I would be doing. I threw it away because I did not want someone else's dream for my life to become my reality. I desired to reach higher. If you are going to reach your potential you will have to remove the labels others place on you.

Too often we allow the labels that others place on us to be our lid. Once a label, a tag, is placed on someone, that typically becomes their limit, if they allow it. Too many people today are living beneath their potential because someone threw a label on their life. "Oh, you are divorced, you will never find happiness again." "I can't believe you lost another job. No one is ever going to hire you." "You are not smart enough to go to college." You see, the list could go on and on. People put these lids on our lives by the labels they give us.

We have all heard the negative labels for too long. You could never do that. That's impossible. You are not good enough. You don't have the right education. Sadly, many of us allow what others have said about us to become our lid. Hear me today, you are more than you think you are. You can do more than you know you can. You have God-sized potential living on the inside of your life. Never let your label become your lid.

DON'T SETTLE FOR A LABEL

There's a story in the Bible about a man named Jacob. Jacob was left all alone in this camp, when a man shows up. The man begins wrestling with him. It was an all night wrestling match. Jacob would NOT let go. The man says, "You have to let go of me – morning is coming." Jacob refuses. The man, who is an angel, then dislocates the hip of Jacob, hoping this would cause him to let go. Still, Jacob held on. Here's what Jacob said, "I will not let go until you bless me." The angel then changes Jacob's name to Israel and blesses him.

What's the significance of the name change? It was all about a new dream and destiny. Israel simply means, you "have fought and won."[7] Jacob means deceiver. Remember Jacob is the one who stole the blessing from his brother Esau. He deceived his father, Isaac, into giving him the blessing of the firstborn. Jacob, now wrestling with an angel, is basically saying, "I did not earn that blessing. Bless me. I want to be changed. I want the real blessing." The angel of the Lord changed his name and, in that moment, his destiny was changed. A new dream was birthed in his spirit.

It does not matter what others say about you. It only matters what God says about you. He wants to give you a new dream and a fresh destiny. God did not create you to live a mediocre life with ordinary dreams. He has breathed His Spirit into you so that you can fulfill the dreams He has placed in your heart. Refuse to wear the label of your

---

[7] https://www.biblestudytools.com/dictionary/israel/

family, classmates, or friends. You have been given the right to dream. Dream big.

DEVIL'S ADVOCATE

I love when I am dreaming and someone says, "Let me play devil's advocate for a moment." Then they proceed to tell me everything wrong with my dreams, ideas, or goals. There are some people who believe their mission in life is to tell you why you can't. I am not sure why anyone would want to even attach themselves to the enemy. I refuse to play the devil's advocate in anyone's life. I want to cheer them on. Push them higher. Encourage them to dream bigger.

Let's just say I was not always the pastor I am today and neither were my brothers. I remember one lady telling my mother, "Your boys will never serve God. They are too bad." For a season we lived under that negative declaration. However, my mother raised Christian young men, all still married, all great parents, all college graduates, and two of the three are pastors. This teacher acted as the devil's advocate. To be honest, I think she may have been the devil's sister, but we did not embrace what she said!

Here's the thing: *Negativity is catchy*. If you are constantly around negative people, it begins to rub off on you. Several years ago we had a great family come to our church. They were so full of life. Some of the most positive people I had ever met. Then they started spending time with one of the most negative people in our church. Do you know what happened? Before long they became negative. They started seeing everything wrong in church, in work, and in life. Guard who you spend time with, because a negative person will rob you of your dream before you ever know it's gone.

Let me say this, some people believe they have the gift of discouragement: "my job is to bring you back to reality." Listen to what the Bible says, "The lips of the godly speak helpful words" (Proverbs 10:32). What Solomon was saying is the ungodly are discouragers, but the godly are always building up those around them. If someone comes to you as the devil's advocate, don't give them a platform.

I also believe this: *Positivity is catchy too*. If you surround yourself with people that are going to lift you, build you and motivate you, before you know it you will be that to others. I believe that is why I am the consummate encourager today. I was not flooded with the most positive statements by those around me growing up. So today I choose to lift other's spirits, encourage their dreams, and unleash their potential.

VOICES IN MY HEAD

It's hard to admit but sometimes I hear voices in my head. They come up every now and then. They are the same words that haunted me as a child. "You are not good enough." "You will never amount to anything." "You can't do it." "Grow up." One of the greatest challenges I have faced in my life is not what is taking place around me, but the battle inside my mind. Those voices peer into my soul.

71

At the end of every message I preach, I will always ask Mary, "What did you think?" I need her encouragement. I can hear from everyone else, "Great job. Awesome message," but I need to hear it from her. She is the closest person to me. Her words matter more than anyone else's. She drowns out the voices in my head. There are many times I finish a message and I hear, "That wasn't good enough. You could have done better." But, just the encouragement of my bride, "That was great," removes every voice in my head.

I think we all hear voices in our head. Yes, they will come from time to time. Many times they will seem like reality. If you don't have someone positive in your life like I do in Mary, you still have God's Word. It is filled with over 7,000 promises. Declare them over your life. Declare, "I am the apple of God's eye." Scream at the top of your lungs, "I am God's masterpiece." Stand on the truth that you are "blessed coming and going."

You see, the enemy wants to rob your dreams, and he will start in your mind. God has given you the right to dream. Don't let the enemy sidetrack you from the dreams God has placed in your heart. Refuse to let the voices in your head keep you from the vision in your heart. You have the right to dream. Dream again.

CLAIM YOUR RIGHT

1. What are the labels that you have embraced that need to be replaced?

2. Where have you settled, where you should have wrestled?

3. Are there negative voices in your life that need to be silenced?

4. What dreams has God placed in your heart?

I declare that God has given me a dream for my life. I claim my right!

THE RIGHT TO BE ACCEPTED

Chapter 7

I have met many people over the years who have felt the stinging rejection of divorce or abandonment. Every person longs to be accepted by someone, anyone. Rejection comes to everyone. It may look different to you than me, but we all face it. It could come from a spouse, parent, child, or friend.

There have been many times over my life that I felt betrayed, belittled and broken. Some of you know that feeling. You poured out your heart and your life in a certain direction, and then, some person said, "I reject you. You don't have what it takes." "Wish I never had you. Wish that you would go away. You're not welcome here." Just because someone has spoken those words over you does not mean you have to allow them into your spirit. You can feel rejected by everyone, but never forget God accepts you.

Peter denied knowing Jesus after he was arrested. He was one of Jesus' closest disciples. After Jesus rose from the dead, He told Mary to "tell everyone that I've risen and go find Peter." I find it really interesting to know that Jesus called out Peter. Why? I believe it's because he wanted Peter to know that he was still accepted. Jesus did not hold on to the hurt. Instead, He gave grace. Peter felt the acceptance of Jesus in his darkest moment. God has given you the right to be accepted.

TOO MANY CHURCHES

As I was preparing to graduate from Bible college, I really believed that God had called me to plant a church in Buffalo, New York – my hometown. I was so excited. I remember going into the library, typing my plan and printing it out on the old dot matrix printer. I called it the "Buffalo Urban Church Planting Project." I knew that God placed the heart to plant a church in my spirit. I spoke to one of our District denominational leaders, shared my heart to plant a church and anxiously waited to see their excitement too. Instead, I was told "there are too many churches in Buffalo." I had this dream from God and that dream was rejected by man. It was a crushing moment in my life.

I knew rejection. It was something I had grown accustomed to, but I never thought anyone would reject the dream God birthed in my spirit. I prayed. I fasted. I believed. Still I was faced with rejection.

There will be well-meaning people in your life that will not be able to see what God is doing in you. They won't accept you or your dream, but thank God you don't need their approval. God's approval is more important than man's applause. Don't allow a rejection to be the end of your story. Keep pushing forward. Trust God.

Sadly, I never planted that church in Buffalo, but when God plants a dream in your heart it will come to life. Thirteen years after God planted that dream in the soil of my spirit, Mary and I planted a church. Not in Buffalo, but in Long Island, New York. The day we launched our church in 2008, I remember the Holy Spirit whispering in my ear, "The dream I gave you 13 years ago was for this moment in your life. I spent the last 13 years preparing you." Whoa. People may never accept the vision God gave to you, but at the right time your Creator will bring it to life.

DELAYED, NOT DENIED

I have learned that if the enemy can get you to lose hope, he can submerge your potential. If he can get you to misplace hope, he will confuse your dreams, goals, and destiny. Sometimes life hits the pause button on our potential. Don't let it define you – let it refine you. Use that season to become who God designed you to be, before you do what He designed you to do.

Hope gets you up in the morning. Hope restores your joy. Hope causes you to stay focused! Hope gives you the strength to keep going! The enemy would like you to spend your whole life living hopeless. Do not surrender your hope! Just because you have not experienced the promise does not mean it is not on its way.

Living on Long Island we know delays. Traffic is the never ending problem. Too many cars, not enough road. All it takes is one accident to cause you to be late. Every car slows down, examines the accident, and then passes the disaster. One accident can back up the traffic for miles, but even though my progress is delayed I will still get to my destination.

In life we all face delays. Most people see a delay as a denial. God has rejected my dream, prayer, goal or ambition. A delay could be God's simple way of preparing you for the next step in your journey. Keep your faith up, hopes high, and dreams alive. Until it's a "no," it's a "not yet." That's how I live each day. I wait patiently for the promise God spoke into my heart. You are accepted by God.

FORGET THE CROWDS

Bartimaeus was a blind beggar sitting on the side of the road near Jericho. He hears that Jesus is coming near him. He had high hopes. He begins to shout, "Son of David, have mercy on me." The people start telling him, "Be quiet." In other words, "Bartimaeus, God will not accept you." Bartimaeus starts yelling louder. He wanted to see and he would not let Hell keep him blind. Jesus hears him and says, "What do you want me to do for you?" He says, "My rabbi, I want to see." Instantly the man could see!

Bartimaeus knew where his hope was. He was not looking for hope in the crowd of people and he wasn't satisfied in his current situation. He did not need their acceptance or approval. He did not let the crowd keep him blind. He rose above the crowd. Never settle for the crowd.

Friend, hell is going to try to rob your hope, usually by the people around you. They are going to try to discourage you. Don't let what people say determine what you see! Allow what God says to determine what you see! Forget the crowds.

One of my favorite professors in Bible College was Dr. David Arnett. He was such an articulate communicator. But I remember something he said in chapel that has stuck with me. He said, "Live to please an audience of one." That was good then and it is good now. You see, if I constantly need people's approval, I will be left disappointed. But, if I know that God accepts me as I am because He created me as I am, I will trust him more and more. Man's applause fades. God's approval lasts eternally.

DON'T HIT SEND

I was seeing this girl, many years ago, long before Mary was ever in the picture (*just want to make that clear*). We were dating for about 4 months when she decided to break up with me. Here's how she did it. She sent me an email. Cold, right? She literally dumped me over the internet. That affected me. For many years I chose to ride solo. I did not want to have any relationship because that was a brutal rejection.

I think, more often than we would like to admit, our past rejections affect our relationship with God. I know it may sound crazy at first, but hear me out. Every time we are rejected by someone, another person pays a price. The person who pays the most is God. We can easily blame God for the divorce or breakup. We can quickly blame God for the loss or mistake. He gets blamed for everyone else's behavior.

Scripture teaches that "God showed his great love for us by sending Christ to die for us while we were still sinners" (Romans 5:8). Notice the last few words. No matter what we face or fail at in life, God will never love us any more or any less than He does at this incredible moment. That's why He sent Jesus to show us that we have the right to be accepted. He accepts us. Damaged goods and all.

This is a hard concept for us to embrace because it is so opposite of how we are. That's why He is God. He does things right, perfectly, all the time. I am sure if God had asked someone for advice, they would have said, "Don't send your son. Those people don't deserve it." That still would not have stopped him. God hit the send button even when we did not deserve it or could ever earn it. As crazy as it sounds, God accepts us as we are, not as He hopes we are.

YOU ARE NEVER TOO FAR

There are a lot of people who roll through life believing that God would not accept them because of how bad they were or are. Nothing could be further from the truth. God's love and acceptance is not based on what we do, it is based on what He has done. His love is greater than any sin you could ever commit.

Three of the most powerful words you can ever hear, "I love you." Love is not an accident. It is a choice! I remember when Mary and I started dating. Within just a few weeks we decided to get married! We are a pretty patient couple. I loved hearing Mary say, "I LOVE YOU" in the early days. In fact, I love hearing it today, probably even more! There is something powerful about I LOVE YOU!

The words I LOVE YOU build 3 things:

- **Commitment**. Love is a choice, but it is also a commitment. Love reveals commitment.

- **Confidence**. When you sense the love of someone, you are not insecure in that relationship. You are confident.

- **Consistency**. Love will build consistency. If a relationship is inconsistent, it really shows there is a love issue.

God's love is no different. His love builds commitment, confidence and consistency for us too. You may need to hear this today: God loves you! Your past can't keep God's love away! Your sins can't keep God's love away! God loves you! He has given you the right to be accepted by Him.

The most famous verse in the Bible says, "For God loved the world so much that he gave his one and only son, so that anyone who believes in him will not perish but have eternal life" (John 3:16). God loves you so much that He wanted to give you real life. He wants you to have purpose. He desires for you to have a life filled with possibilities! He wants you to sense his acceptance.

1 John 4:9: "God showed how much he loved us by sending his one and only Son." God's love and acceptance is not based on what you do, it is based on what He has done.

CHOOSE TO BE ACCEPTED

Maybe you feel far from God. Today is your day to lay aside every excuse you could ever make and just accept His love.

Maybe you are reading this book and you have never accepted Jesus into your heart. Today would be a great day to have a fresh start, a new beginning. If that's you, would you simply say this prayer with me ... "Lord Jesus, I repent of my sins. I ask you to forgive me. Be my Lord and Savior. In Jesus name we pray, Amen." If you prayed that prayer I want to welcome you to the family of God.

Email me: todd@toddbishop.tv. Tell me what God has just done in your life. Then get plugged into a great church where you can grow closer to Jesus. I believe God will take you places you could never imagine.

CLAIM YOUR RIGHT

1. When have you felt the most rejected or unaccepted?

2. Do you look for the approval of people or God?

3. Are there times when you wish you never "hit the send button?"

4. Have you made a decision to start a relationship with Jesus? When? Where?

I declare that I am fully embraced by God and His love for me is eternal. I claim my right!

THE RIGHT TO FEEL PAIN

Chapter 8

Pain is one of the greatest teachers. It's the teacher that no one wants, but everyone needs. Pain has taught me many things over the years. It has taught me what I should never do again. It has taught me lessons that I would never have learned without it. It is okay to feel pain and to experience hurt.

I remember arriving late to a basketball game that I was playing in. I must have been about 10 years old. My mother did everything to get me there, but with her work schedule it was often challenging for her during the week. Long story short, as soon as I arrived, the coach put me right in. I found myself standing all alone at half court, received the pass, and went in for an easy layup. There was one problem. I went to the wrong hoop. Coach called a timeout. The other team was laughing at me. Parents were laughing. My team was angry. Coach said, "Todd, we are going *that* way," as he pointed to the other hoop. I was embarrassed. Needless to say, it never happened again.

But that moment on the basketball court taught me something that I will never forget. It is okay to feel hurt and pain. It is not always easy. In fact, it is one of the hardest schoolmasters. Difficulty teaches you how push through your pain and how to handle hurt.

I was so mad at my mom at the end of the game. I did not even want to speak with her. I was angry that she worked late. I was upset that she made me late to the game. I was hurt. But, my mother asked me one question on the way home, and it was this, "What did you learn?" My first response was, "Not to be late." Then she asked me again, "What did you learn?" I thought for a moment and said, "If I am late I have to ask coach which way we are going." "That's right," she responded. My mother taught me at an early age that hurt and pain can teach you to ask the right questions.

PAIN HAS A PURPOSE

I am sure you are thinking, "A purpose? Yea, I know the purpose. It is to destroy me." Hear this: suffering, pain, problems, or sickness will not destroy you, but they will define your life! They will make you stronger and more able to do what God has called you to do. Your pain is always a platform to your potential!

Scripture reads, "We can rejoice, too, when we run into problems and trials, for we know that *they help us* develop endurance" (Romans 5:3). Paul is reminding us that pain helps us. It will help us become all that God desires of us! Pain helps us clear away what isn't important to "help us" focus on what matters! I have heard it said,

"You can't have a testimony without a test. You can't have a message without a mess." How true is that?

Every person faces pain. It does not matter what they share on social media or how they appear in public. No one is exempt from it. To be honest, pain is a right that God has given to us. If you were not hard-wired to feel pain, you could cut your arm off, think you were okay, and bleed to death. God has placed within us the ability to feel pain to protect us. It is a gift!

Rick Warren said, "God never wastes a hurt."[8] That has spoken to me since I heard it. God will not cause your pain, but He will often use it. If you are experiencing pain or suffering right now, let me give you some important, tweetable principles:

- Suffering **doesn't** mean God has turned his back on you.
- Suffering **doesn't** always come because of sin & disobedience.
- Suffering **doesn't** give you permission to give up.
- Suffering **often** places us exactly where God wants us to be.

What is suffering? Suffering is really when someone is going through something that appears to be more than they can handle. Have you ever been there? I know I have. But, the word that we have to focus on is *appears*. It appears to be more than we can handle. God would not have allowed it if He did not have a reason for it.

---

[8] http://pastorrick.com/devotional/english/your-pain-often-reveals-god-s-purpose

PAIN HAS A SEASON

This is the part of suffering we all love, when the pain ends! Are you going through something? I have good news for you. It is time to declare that season is over in your life. Your spiritual winter is passing and spring is coming. Get ready, because God has the final word in our pain.

The Bible teaches, "News about him spread as far as Syria, and people soon began bringing to him all who were sick. And whatever their sickness or disease, or if they were demon possessed or epileptic or paralyzed--he healed them all." (Matthew 4:24). That is what God wants to do in your situation right now. He wants to heal it. He wants to heal you.

Are you suffering with sickness? God can handle it. Are you stuck in your past? God can give you a fresh start. Do you find yourself living with relational dysfunction? God can restore. Have your children run away from God? Never forget He still welcomes the prodigal. Living with fear? God can flood you with incredible strength and courage. I believe God wants to do something in this moment in your life. He wants to heal your pain. You have the right to feel pain and God has the right to heal it.

What has caused your greatest pain? Big question. But this is a divine moment with you and God. Write it down in the margin of this book right now. Confess your pain to Him and watch how quickly He responds. Don't let the pain of your heart become the story of your life. Your season of pain is turning into a lifetime of victory.

I AIN'T BROKEN

There are some people who face, what seems to be, a lifetime of pain and they begin to believe the lie that they are "broken goods." I grew up with those thoughts. I thought that I was broken goods. Our family faced a lot of challenges growing up. I carried that into college and beyond. It was like difficulty was the U-Haul attached to my life story. Then one day I said, "Enough is enough." I made a declaration in my mid-20s. I declared, "I ain't broken. I am God's masterpiece. He doesn't make crap." True story.

For years I believed the lies in my mind. I believed I was broken goods and nothing would ever change. I had hopes and dreams, but I never believed that God would ever use me. After all, I was just broken goods. It all changed that day I started declaring what I was, not what I thought I was! I am God's masterpiece. That became the mantra of my life. I declared Ephesians 2:10 wherever I went. I use it with teenagers to remind them they are made for more. I use it with adults to push them beyond their pain.

You are not broken goods. Broken is what happens around you, but it does not have to happen in you. It is your right to feel pain and hurt, but don't let it break your spirit. You are not broken. You are God's masterpiece. He has a plan and purpose for your life in the pain, through the pain, and beyond the pain.

It took me years to realize that I was not broken goods that no one wanted or could ever love. Don't wait your lifetime to realize that God did not make a mistake when He made you.

IT'S OKAY TO NOT BE OKAY

There are days I am not okay. I still wrestle, like everyone else, with the pains of my past. However, I am so glad that we don't have to be okay all the time. Early in my faith, I thought I could not show my pain or hurt. I was under the impression that faith was about denying your pain, but in reality, faith is best seen when you embrace your pain.

Early in my ministry I thought that I had to have it all together. I could never show any insecurity, doubt, or worry. I had to be the pastor all the time. Now, as I have gotten older, I have realized that you lead others through your strengths, but you connect through your setbacks. The common denominators of every person ever created are that we all have weaknesses, we all face challenges, and we all experience problems.

Several years ago I had a battle with anxiety. It was one of the most difficult seasons I have ever faced in my life. I was not prepared for this nine-month journey. I lost 25 pounds. I had a difficult time doing anything. I tried my hardest to ignore it. That was almost impossible, but I tried. Mary was so patient as I walked through the journey. I was not okay.

As a pastor, I used to tell people who were sick, "Get to church. God is there. He will heal you." Now I was the one who did not even want to go to church. My mind was winning the battle, until I stopped allowing my thoughts to control my life. Here's what I have learned: *You will never win the battles in your life, until you first win the battles in your mind.* That journey taught me compassion and patience. Two things that were not as strong as I hoped, prior to this moment in my life. The pain of anxiety taught me.

One Sunday, I stood in front of our church, and I told the audience I was struggling with panic attacks and anxiety on a regular basis. I shared with them that the beauty of God is that "it's okay to not be okay." It was healing and therapeutic for me. Something great started to happen. Dozens and dozens of people approached me after that Sunday and said, "I thought I was the only one." I never realized that sharing my pain could be someone else's prescription! Our church realized that I am not okay and that gave them the freedom to not be ok. It's a God-given right!

NEVER LET PAIN WIN

I have discovered that those who succeed in anything have the amazing ability to hold on, to never quit, and to push through their challenges! Don't let the pain win. Work your way through it. Don't deny it, but also don't focus on it. 2 Corinthians 4:1 declares, "Therefore, since God in his mercy has given us this new way, **we never give up.**" If you truly want to experience real joy in this life, you have to push through every problem, outlast any obstacle, and succeed over every setback.

Let me ask you a question: "What do you do when life ruins your plans?" You know, when things don't go the way you planned. When it seems as though God has responded in the exact opposite way you hoped He would. What do you do? First, recognize *pain is part of the growing process*. It's part of the process none of us like, but it still pushes us to grow. Don't let the pain you feel stop you. The enemy would love to use the pain to force you to hit the pause button on life. Don't allow pain to win.

Second, understand that *everything in life is temporary*. Nobody is designed to live forever, and nothing is designed to endure forever. Everything is temporary. Even pain. The pain you are experiencing today will not last forever. Don't let temporary difficulties derail long-term destinies. That loss or hurt is real, but work through them.

I also believe *complaining only prolongs the pain*. The more you talk about it, the more you feel the agony of it. Don't just cry over what you have lost, celebrate what you have left. I know some things are traumatic. There are moments that are so hurtful that it's hard to move forward. But, you can't let your pain keep you from your destiny. Get up every day and declare, "Today is going to be a great day. Today is going to be the day I get better, become more, and get through what life has brought me to."

Finally, realize the best thing you can ever do is ***never give up***. Don't quit. No matter what you are facing today, choose to believe, because nothing is impossible with God! Take a step of faith! Trust God in all things and you will see His hand on your life!

If God could speak to Moses through a burning bush, then God can speak to you. If God could heal a man with leprosy, then God can heal you. If God could part the Red Sea and the Jordan River, then God can part the rivers of adversity for you. No matter what you are facing, face it with faith. Run out your front door and scream at the top of your lungs: "Nothing is impossible with God."

Remember, you have the right to feel pain, and God has the right to heal your pain. Don't deny your hurt. Embrace it. Confess it. Watch God heal it!

CLAIM YOUR RIGHT

1. What has been your most painful moment?

2. Have you ever been stuck in your pain? Why or why not?

3. Where have you felt like "broken goods?"

4. Do you truly believe that nothing is impossible with God?

I declare that my pain has a reason and a season! I will not get discouraged or be defeated!

THE RIGHT TO HOPE

Chapter 9

I am addicted to hope. It's true. I have a hat that I wear all the time. It says, "HOPE DEALER," on it, in all caps. It's a stand out for sure. No matter where I go, someone will always mention my hat. It's a conversation piece, but it is also something I want to do all the time. I want to deal some hope.

A good friend of mine, Danny, struggled for years with addictive behaviors, but through God's grace he has been clean for many years. I remember shooting a video with him for our church. He said this incredible line, "I went from being a hopeless dope dealer to a dopeless hope dealer." That was the birth of a movement in my spirit. The Hope Dealer was born. Every person has a right to hope.

The family struggling to find a place to live has the right to hope. The individual with a bad medical report has the right to hope. The parents trying to get their child off drugs has the right to hope. Hope wakes you up in the morning. It keeps you from going insane when you are walking through hell. It stirs your spirit to keep dreaming and believing.

DON'T BURY YOUR HOPE

The Bible declares, "Hope deferred makes the heart sick, but a dream fulfilled is a tree of life" (Proverbs 13:12). I have learned that if the enemy can get you to bury your hope, he can bury your potential. If he can get you to lose your hope, he will bury your dreams, goals, and destiny. Don't bury your hopes in the casket of unanswered prayers, delayed dreams, or denied goals. The coffin of hopelessness will keep you from enjoying your life of purpose! Don't give up your rights of hope.

There have been many times in my spiritual life when my hopes were attacked. Dreams that I had remained buried, but I chose to see with eyes of hope. I remember several years ago our church was $42,000 behind budget and it was almost the end of the year. I was anxious, overwhelmed, and worried. I had no clue how God was going to work his miracle wand. Mary and I kept hoping, believing, and praying.

At that time we were a portable church. We were meeting in a movie theater. We would set up and tear down our church, lobby, and kids space every week. We were spending about $60,000 on rent for 4 hours of usage on a Sunday morning. I had no idea where God would provide, but I never lost hope.

Out of the blue, I received a call from a pastor who said they had their last service and wanted to see if I would be interested in buying their church building. This was probably the worst time to buy a building, but I said ok. I went and he took me on a tour of the building. Long story short, he showed us the Comparative Market Analysis for the building. The value: $864,000. That was impossible for us, but even still he said, "Make us an offer." We offered them $225,000. Three weeks later they accepted our offer. That's why you can never bury your hope; because God has an incredible track record. You have been given the right to hope.

STAY EAGER

What drives your life? That's a great question, right? In order to live with hope you have to stay eager. Eager for what? A lot of people are driven by things – popularity, power, position.

There will always be people EAGER to make a bigger profit, climb the corporate ladder, or discover a cure for a disease and none of those things are wrong. In fact, God may have put a drive in you for that, but we should stay eager for what matters most.

Solomon, King David's son, told us, "Whoever pursues righteousness and unfailing love will find life, righteousness, and honor" (Proverbs 21:21). This incredible passage teaches us several principles. Don't miss the story behind the story!

Solomon said pursue two things:

- *Righteousness* – honesty of life or integrity.

- *Love* – living life with goodness and kindness to all people.

Solomon basically said, STAY EAGER for those two things and if you are you will get three benefits:

- *Life* – you will discover what it means to really live.

- *Righteousness* –if you are a person of integrity God, will surround you with people of integrity.

- *Honor* – people will look up to you; your reputation will precede you.

Solomon was telling us to stay eager for what is most important and God will bring you everything you are looking for. God has given us the right to hope and that helps us stay focused on what really matters.

DELETE SELF-DESTRUCTIVE THOUGHTS

The Bible says it this way, "As a person *thinks* within himself, so is he." (Proverbs 23:7 - NASV). You are a product of your thoughts. The Hebrew word in this passage for "thinks" comes from the original word, שָׁעַר (**shaar**), "*to estimate, to calculate.*"[9] Therefore, the verse is best written, 'For as one that *calculates* within himself, so is he.' It is

---

[9] Strong's Concordance. http://biblehub.com/hebrew/8176.htm
104

a process of thinking over and over again. So your *thoughts* help determine your *trajectory*!

Hit the "delete" button on the thoughts that have held you in bondage! I may not know exactly what you are facing, but I do know something about negative words versus positive words. I have had my share of each spoken into my life. I can't focus on what others say about me, the situations I face, or even my own negative thoughts. I have to look to God and what He says about me, how much He cares for me, and how He helps me overcome anything in my life.

I think, many times, we are self-toxic, because we repeat the negative thoughts, words, or images over and over again in our heads. Delete those negative self-thoughts. Refuse to let those thoughts take root.

All the experts told a young man named *Emmitt Smith,* who grew up in a low-income family and lived in public housing, that, at 5 feet 9 inches tall, he was too small and too slow to play in the National Football League.[10] But, Emmitt knew how to hit the "delete" button and went on to rush for more yardage than any player in NFL history.[11] Emmitt has won three Super Bowls and is now enshrined at the NFL hall of fame.

Don't tell yourself you can't, because with God "you can do all things." There is nothing that can limit your potential but you.

---

[10] Joseph, Paul. Emmitt Smith. Abdo & Daughters. 1997. Print.
[11] http://www.espn.com/nfl/history/leaders/_/stat/rushlead

Sometimes you have to do what David did and encourage yourself in the Lord.[12]

KEEP PRAISING IN THE HALLWAY.

Hope helps you realize that some doors need to close and that we have to wait for God to open the right doors for us. What do you do when you are waiting? You praise God in the hallway!

David wrote, "I will praise the LORD at all times. I will constantly speak his praises" (Psalm 34:1). We celebrate God when we are experiencing the greatest of days and even when we are in the hallway of waiting. Praise is not determined by our circumstances. It is established by our hope in God's plan.

Several years ago I had the privilege to meet Nik Wallenda. He's the man who walked across the Grand Canyon and the Niagara Falls on a 2-inch high wire. That is freaking ridiculous. For 200 years, eight generations, their family has been walking on high wires. Nik leaves the safety of the one side of the high wire, and while he is crossing, he does nothing but praise God until he arrives safely on the other side.

The best thing you can do when you are in the hallway of waiting is PRAISE God. Hope in the middle of Hell is what keeps you going. The Apostle Paul said it this way, "Be thankful in all circumstances, for this is God's will for you who belong to Christ Jesus" (1 Thessalonians 5:18). Keep praising God in the hallway!

---

[12] 1 Samuel 30:6

Don't lose your joy. Refuse to allow your hallway moments to keep you from walking through the next open door. Praise God while you wait and watch how He unlocks your next season.

CHOOSE TO SEE OPPORTUNITIES

It is hard to see the opportunities when there are obstacles all around us. It's all about how we see what we are going through or experiencing. I believe God can turn any obstacle into an opportunity! That's our hope.

Jesus. He is placed on the cross. At first glance this could be seen as the greatest obstacle He ever faced, but Jesus knew that His obstacle would lead to our opportunity! Psalm 5:8: "Lead me in the right path, O LORD, or my enemies will conquer me. Make your way plain for me to follow." One translation finishes that verse, "Remove the obstacles." God has the amazing ability to take an obstacle and use it to build us, motivate us, and direct us. The reality is there are no obstacles with God, only opportunities.

Lazarus was dead. That's a problem. A pretty big obstacle, but Jesus declares, "Lazarus sickness will not end in death. It happened for a purpose." In other words, death isn't an *obstacle* for me, it is an *opportunity* for God to be praised.

You may be facing what seems to be your greatest obstacle. Hold on. God is about to turn that situation or season around. Keep your hopes high. Don't let life beat you down. Wake up each day knowing that God loves you, is with you and is always for you.

I love what the Psalmist declared, "Yet I am confident *I will see the LORD's goodness* while I am here in the land of the living" (Psalm 27:3). That's hope. You have been given the right to hope. Don't forfeit it. Stay confident. God will bring your through what life has brought you to.

Get your hopes high. Don't settle for the lies of the enemy. Focus on the reality that God has brought you this far. If you are not dead, then God is not done. Celebrate how far you have come and get ready for what is next! Claim your right to hope.

CLAIM YOUR RIGHT

1. What drives you & keeps you eager (going)?

2. What hopes are you still hanging on to?

3. Is there a hallway you are currently in? Are you ready to get out?

4. List what you are thankful for. Praise God

I declare that I am free to hope,
growing in faith and sure of my future.
I claim my right!

THE RIGHT TO CHANGE

Chapter 10

Several years ago, we had a family leave the church that was incredibly close to us. We spent a lot of time together. Our children were best friends, and Mary and I both got along with this couple. It was truly a blessing to have friends who you could just be you around. Sadly, the family, out of the blue, just left the church. They never said anything to us. They simply left. It was very tough for us, but it was even tougher for our children. That was the first time Malachi, our oldest, had anyone leave the church that he was close to. It was difficult for him.

Later, we were told that they left because "Mary and I had changed." They went on to say, "You are not the same people that led the church. You are different." I had a very simple, clear response, "Thank you." To be honest, I was glad that we were different. Mary and I were growing, changing, and becoming who God designed us to be.

Change. Nobody likes it, but everybody needs it. That's why God has given us the right to change, to become someone better. We were not designed to just take up space, we were designed to live. That requires change! As you grow closer to your destiny, change will be part of the process. Embrace change.

If you want to become all that God handcrafted you for, then you will have to be open to adjustments. There will be some things that you will have to stop doing, and there will be things that you will need to start doing. Change is part of the process.

Mary and I had to discover that not everyone who starts with you will be able to finish with you. I say it this way, "Those who don't grow with you can't go with you." This was something we had to learn, because we wanted to keep everyone happy. But, as our church was growing we had to grow too. That meant change!

DON'T STAY WHERE YOU ARE

So many people just stay where they are because they are afraid to change. But, I have discovered, if I stay where I am, I will never get where I want to be. I have to constantly make adjustments in my life.

One of the people that Mary and I are so proud of is Gina. We have known her since she was a teenager. There was always something different about her. Gina is incredibly gifted and talented. On the outside, you could think that she never faced difficulty, challenge, or pain. But, her story is similar to mine. She knows dysfunction and heartbreak. Gina has experienced a lot in her life, but she refused to stay where she was. Mary and I saw potential in this young lady. We brought her in as a '$100 per week intern.' She excelled. We brought her back the next summer. The rest is history. Gina currently serves as the Executive Pastor of our church at 29 years old and we could not be prouder. Knowing the depth of her history proves the strength of her destiny.

Gina did what I am asking you to do. Don't stay where you are. She could have walked around defeated, but she chose to rise above her challenges. You too can choose to live defeated or live victorious. It all comes down to how much change you are willing to make. Don't get stuck in the rut of routine. Don't accept a status quo life. Get up. Do something. Change.

THOUGHTS CREATE CHANGE

One of the major things the enemy will do in your life is change your focus. If he can get you to focus your thoughts on everything bad, negative, and not-so-good, you will have a hard time seeing what God is doing right in your life. You cannot change your life until you first change your thoughts!

The enemy is the master of misdirection, misinformation, and misleading. That's why he fights so hard for your thoughts, because your thoughts direct your trajectory. The Bible reveals, "Be careful what you think, because **your thoughts run your life**" (Proverbs 4:23 – NCV). Did you catch that? Your thoughts run your life. They set the course, speed and destiny. So if the enemy can change your thoughts – he changes your destiny.

This is powerful. Your mindset matters. Your thoughts matter. The enemy may be able to plant negative thoughts in your mind, but you determine whether or not they take root. When a negative thought comes in, it is like a weed and it chokes out the good stuff. What do you do with weeds? You rip them out. What should you do with negative thoughts? Rip them out!

Check out this verse: "Roll your works upon the Lord [commit and trust them wholly to Him; He *will cause your thoughts to become agreeable to His will*, and] so shall *your plans be established and succeed*" (Proverbs 16:3 - AMP). In other words, get your thoughts on God, trust Him, and He will re-align your thoughts. Notice what happens next – "your plans will be established and succeed." Notice, you cannot have success without first having the right thoughts. Change all starts with the right thoughts. Your thoughts create change.

SHIFT YOUR FOCUS

Asaph was a Levite appointed by King David to help manage worship. He wrote 12 of the Psalms. He was facing a difficult time in his life, he cried out to the Lord. He said things like, "I am too distressed to pray," and "I am overwhelmed." He also asked questions like, "Has the Lord rejected me?" and "Has God forgotten me?" Asaph was wrestling with some pretty negative thoughts about life, what he was experiencing, and what he is going through. But, then he wrote, "But then I recall all you have done, O LORD; I remember your wonderful deeds of long ago. They are constantly in my thoughts. I cannot stop thinking about your mighty works" (Psalm 77:11-12).

Asaph changed what he was thinking about, recalibrated his focus, and replaced the negative thoughts about what he was experiencing with what God has done. Hear this today: *"You may not be able to stop a negative thought from coming, but you can stop it from staying."* That may be worth the whole book! How did Asaph do that? He replaced the negative thoughts with positive ones! He shifted his focus. He remembered all the good things.

You see, all of us are going to have difficult times. Every person faces challenging moments and yes, even negative thoughts. But, recall "all that the Lord has done." When you are able to get your focus off what has gone wrong or what is going wrong – and remember God has been really good – your outlook begins to change.

PREPARE FOR THE HATERS

Not everyone is going to celebrate where you are going! There are going to be a lot of people that praise us, celebrate us, or honor us that are not sincere. Their motives are not right. As you change, not everyone is going to embrace it. Honestly, many people are going to attack it.

I was so excited about being asked to be on the international "Praise The Lord" program on TBN (a Christian television station). It was something I never expected. As someone who grew up with feelings that I would never amount to anything it became an exclamation point on the changes God had done in my life. Afterward, one pastor came up to me, gave me a hug, and told me I did a great job. But, just a few moments later, that same pastor publicly belittled me. It hurt deep.

Haters come in all shapes and sizes. Some haters are 'in your face' and others 'behind your back.' No matter where it comes from it will still hurt. As you change and discover the power of who you are, the haters are gonna hate. Don't let that keep you from your right to change.

Several years ago, Mary and I had the privilege to become partners with Joel and Victoria Osteen. To date, it is still one of the greatest honors in our ministry. Joel and Victoria are two of the most genuine people we have ever met. When you have a conversation with them, they make you feel like you are the most important person in the room. But, the moment we became part of their Champions Network of churches, the haters came out of everywhere. We were criticized, discredited, and insulted by various 'religious' people. It was hard to take. We got nailed in text messages, emails, and social media rants. But we believed that God had opened up this incredible friendship. The Osteens, Lakewood Church, and Champions Network have helped us grow our church and our leadership in so many ways. Our circle changed. It got bigger and better.

Here's what I have learned: *Haters are just jealous*! They are jealous of your open doors, opportunities and relationships. Most of the people who attack others struggle with their own identity. Don't respond to the haters. Ignore them. They did not create your destiny and they cannot stop it.

Some relationships will need to change. Not everyone that helped you get where you are today will be the ones to help you get to where God wants you to be tomorrow. Don't be afraid to change your relationship circle. Yes, it may create some jealous haters, but never underestimate the power of the right friendships!

FULL REDEMPTIVE POTENTIAL

I believe that there is nothing in your life that can restrict your potential. Nothing that you experience or go through, good or bad, can stop you from accomplishing your full redemptive potential! Your full redemptive potential is what you have come through, what you are going through, but, ultimately, what God has called you to. Every person is filled with full redemptive potential.

There are many days that I say to myself, because it's okay to talk to yourself from time to time, "Todd, can you believe how far you have come?" And every time I answer myself, "No, Todd, I cannot." That's how you know it has to be God. I cannot explain how I got where I am or do what I do. My wife, Mary, says it all the time, "It's a miracle that you came out halfway normal." Kidding. She does not say it like that, but she knows my whole story and celebrates with me

119

the hand of God on my life. That's full redemptive potential. I am living it.

God wants you to live in your sweet spot. In fact, He made you to live there and push against the urge to settle and coast. He wants you to strive and work hard to become all that He designed you to be. But that requires change, or what I call, full redemptive potential.

You still have time to live your potential, where you are, right now. There is still time for you to do that thing that God has called you to. You are never too old and you are not too young to make the changes necessary to become all that He designed you for. Don't just sit around! Choose to discover that thing God made you for and live it out with 150% of your energy.

Let me give you some Biblical examples of full redemptive potential or change:

☐ Moses was called *from* Egypt, *through* Jethro's house (his father in law), *to* become the leader of 1-2 million Israelites traveling through the wilderness.

☐ Joseph was called *from* his father's house, *through* the pathway of prison, *to* lead over Egypt.

☐ The Israelites were called *from* slavery, *through* the wilderness, *to* the Promised Land.

☐ Samuel was called *from* being Eli's servant, *through* growing up in the presence of the Lord, *to* become the priest for all of Israel.

☐ Nehemiah was called *from* being the King's Cupbearer, *through* rebuilding the wall of Jerusalem, *to* raising up a group of spiritual leaders.

What about Jesus' disciples? Matthew was called *from* being a tax collector. Luke was called *from* the medical profession. Peter, Andrew, James, and John were called *from* their family fishing business. They all went *through* the Ministry School of Jesus and ended up leading the early followers of Christ, establishing the faith that many of us embrace here today! The lived full redemptive potential.

It all starts with what God has called you *from* – that's about change. All of our sins, alcohol addiction, cheating, abuse, foul language, religion-bound thoughts and actions, selfishness, lying, etc. The list can go on. Others, like me, were called from one thing to another thing. First, I wanted to be an accountant. I took several advanced courses in accounting during my junior and senior years of high school, but, in the middle of my senior year, I felt the call of God to do ministry. God had something different in store for me.

BEND, DON'T BREAK

My Senior Year of high school I received the "Future Young Business Man of the Year" Award. When they introduced me, the announcement went something like this: "It is our privilege to award Todd Bishop the 'Future Young Business Man of The Year' award. Todd will be attending Central Bible College in Springfield, MO to study – {*there was a long pause – wait for it*} theology. I guess that's right? Congratulations, Todd."

You see, I had my plans, but, God's potential for my life was much more powerful. God sent me *through* Bible College and, fast-forward to today, God has called me *to* Long Island and *Church Unleashed* to lead others in unleashing their 'full redemptive potential.' I believe that Mary and I are now just scratching the surface of our potential and I believe the same is true for you. Together we can reach our potential and change the world!

Too many people fight off God's plans! They want to do their thing and they forget that God has bigger plans than they could ever imagine! Did you ever think about why God put palm trees in the Caribbean? I have. Because when the storms of that region come, they can bend to the severe winds. Imagine if the mighty oaks of the Northeastern United States were there; they would break. When it comes to our plans, we must choose to be like a palm tree – we bend to God's plans and purposes.

Where do you need to make some changes? Is there a part of your life that you know needs to be changed? Don't wait another day. Make a change today. You were made for this moment! Get up. Get going.

YOU WERE MADE FOR MORE

Never underestimate the power of your destiny. You were not created to live an average, ordinary life. You were called to live the life that God has called you to. But you have to embrace your right to change, because, without change, you may never experience your potential. The Bible declares, "No eye has seen, no ear has heard, and no mind has imagined what God has prepared for those who love him" (1 Corinthians 2:9). Paul is reminding his listeners that they were made for more. Friend, hear me today, you are made for more. Don't let your pain, past, perversions, or problems keep you from your potential.

You can feel like you are living a train wreck story, but don't cave in, change. Make the adjustments that you need to be the person God constructed you to be. There is a God-breathed destiny hardwired into your spirit. Refuse to believe the lies of the enemy that you "can never" or "will never." No, you are a child of the Most High God, framed with a function, designed with a destiny, and prepared with a purpose.

You were made for more. Keep pushing the limits on your faith. Refuse to stall out! Live life full throttle. Don't hold back. Push through the pain. Claim your right to change and become who you were made to be.

CLAIM YOUR RIGHT

1. Are there things that you need to change in your life right now?

2. Have you been living your full redemptive potential?

3. In what areas of your life are you breaking instead of bending?

4. What do you believe God has called you to?

I declare that I will live my full redemptive potential!

EPILOGUE

Several years ago I was in the final stages of hosting a Youth Leadership Conference for our region. I was extremely excited. I had an incredible keynote speaker and breakout sessions planned. I had started preparations a year before. The event was a week away when I received a letter from a denominational leader who was critical of our event because it was a few weeks away from theirs. I was called a "lone ranger" and told that I was not a "team player." I had received criticism in the past, but this one cut deep. After all, I did not know about their event when I scheduled mine. I was so hurt.

To add insult to injury, I received more letters from other denominational leaders that they were told not to support our event. I could not believe it. I was trying to do something good and I was being attacked. I had every right to host my own leadership event. This was a very difficult moment in my ministry.

I made the decision to cancel our event. I called the individual who sent me a letter and rallied his 'friends' to ban my event. I did not send him a letter, but shared my heart. I had a conversation. I informed him that I was cancelling my event because I did not want to have a conflict with an organization that I love. He said, "Thank you." To be honest, not much else was said.

Why do I share that? Because, at the moment I received that letter, I was driven backwards to every criticism, negative word or mistreatment that I had experienced before. You see, just because God brings you through something, does not mean you are scarless. I have scars. The wounds have healed, but the scars have remained. You may be finishing this book, claiming your rights and ready for a brighter tomorrow, but never forget how far you have come. Never forget what you have been through. I won't. To be honest, I can't.

The enemy will throw in your path a trigger - something that causes you to regress to a former season. All throughout my life I have faced many triggers. Things that brought memories to the surface that I had forgotten. Statements that were said to me come out of nowhere. I wrestle with the pains of the past, but I don't wrestle defeated. I wrestle knowing that no matter what I face, I win. It took me a long time to get to that point. I am still working on it.

I kept those letters for many years. They served as reminders of what others have said about me. They did not discourage me. They caused me to be more determined. There have been many letters, emails, and

128

conversations that have hurt me deeply, but I am not going to give someone else control of my rights.

No matter what you are experiencing never forget that God has more before you than the enemy has behind you. The enemy wants to keep you looking backwards, because he wants you to take your eyes off of your destiny. But, God has more in front of you. Keep looking forward. Resist the urge to regress.

The Bible declares, *"the Spirit who lives in you is greater than the spirit who lives in the world."*[13] What does that mean? It means that God has more strength for you than you even think you have, because God is empowering your life. God has given you the right to be loved, the right to be you, the right to be wrong, the right to be heard, the right to be respected, the right to dream, the right to be accepted, and the right to hope. Here's the great news: He gives you the strength to face any obstacle.

In Deuteronomy 28, Moses is talking about what happens when you fully obey God. Listen to the opening thoughts of Moses: "If you fully obey the LORD your God and carefully keep all his commands that I am giving you today, the LORD your God will set you high above all the nations of the world." He is going to set you high above, not just individuals, but, nations, and there is only one thing He asks. Just follow Him, obey Him, and He will take you to a higher level.

---

[13] 1 John 4:4. New Living Translation.

The great thing about God is that He doesn't just send you to your destiny, but He goes with you to your destiny!

Listen to the blessings ...

- Your city blessed.

- Your children blessed.

- Your occupation blessed.

- Your income blessed.

- Your future blessed.

When you listen to God you will overcome every attack and setback to experience a lifetime of His blessings!

Here are the promises:

- Your enemies can't defeat you.

- Everything you do will be blessed.

- You will have a solid foundation.

- Your work will have God's direction.

- You will have all you need and then some.

Listen to this: "If you carefully obey them, the LORD will make you the head and not the tail, and you will always be on top and never at the bottom." Do not abdicate your spiritual rights. Claim what God has promised.

For years, I lived claiming the wrong rights. Today, I walk in the confidence that comes from Jesus. There is not a weekend that goes by that Mary and I don't say, "It is such an honor to love and lead our church." We repeat that often because we know where we come from, who we were, but , most importantly, whose we are. We don't walk in our spiritual rights with cockiness, but with confidence. Scripture reads, "So let us come boldly to the throne of our gracious God. There we will receive his mercy, and we will find grace to help us when we need it most" (Hebrews 4:16). We come with a boldness knowing that God has our best intentions at heart.

My daughter, Abigayl, was moved to give her entire life savings in our Miracle Offering Sunday. It was $17.34. She had scrounged every penny. She was so upset that she forgot her offering on that Sunday. I told her it was not an issue and I would bring it to the office. We asked our church to write down the miracle they were believing God for on their envelopes with their gift. So, Abigayl wrote down, "I want a dog." This would be a huge miracle because I don't want a dog. I came home from work that day and she asked, "So, when are we getting the dog." Abigayl believed that if she planted that seed she would reap her miracle. Needless to say, she is probably going to get that dog. Why? Because there is no way I could ever say no to that kind of faith.

Believe today that your loving Heavenly Father wants to unleash favor, blessing, abundance, and miracles on your life. He responds to faith. Choose to believe.

My desire is to pump you up. It is to fill you with a new level of faith, to inspire you to believe, to dream, and to live in your God-given rights! Don't settle! Claim your rights! They have been placed there by God!

Live the human right!

I WANT TO HEAR FROM YOU

I know that every person has a story. That story matters to them, but it also matters to me. Please feel free to share your story with me. I would love to hear about how God is working in your life or even about the struggles you are experiencing.

I believe that your best days are still in front of you. Keep your eyes on God and He will take you places you could never imagine in your wildest dreams.

To contact me, write to:

Todd Bishop
83 Shirley Court
Commack, NY 11725

Or email me:

todd@toddbishop.tv

You can also visit my website, www.toddbishop.tv, for inspirational readings and blogs.

I will be praying for you. I look forward to connecting with you!

ABOUT THE AUTHOR

Todd Bishop serves as **Lead Pastor** of **CHURCH UNLEASHED**, along with Mary, his wife, which they started in 2008. They had one goal – plunder Hell and populate Heaven. Their vision is to establish faith communities across Long Island to reach the 3 million people that call it home.

In 2009, Todd was recognized by the Assemblies of God as one of their *25 Groundbreaking Church Planters*. He was also honored during the 2009 General Council of the Assemblies of God with an *Award of Excellence* for his efforts in Church Planting. Todd was awarded the distinction of *"Young Alumni of the Year"* from Central Bible College in 2010.

In 2014, Hicksville, New York showered Todd with numerous awards and citations for the work that he has been doing in the city. Community, civic, religious, and political leaders from the area have recognized Todd's love for Long Island.

In 2015, Todd received the prestigious "Empowering Long Island Award" at Madison Square Garden from the Empowerment Summit Committee. This award was given to recognize Todd's incredible work in the non-profit sector that has helped empower people to become all that they are designed to be.

Todd & Mary live in Long Island, NY with their three amazing children, **Malachi**, **Abigayl** and **Bethany**.